Language for the Eye

an anthology of

Deaf Writing & Publication

Edited by

George Montgomery

CONTENTS

Prologue
Dedication
George Montgomery & Gordon Davidson | Introduction: Publishing & The Deaf | 1
Don Reed | A Deaf Poetess | 4
Dorothy Miles | Language for the Eye | 6
Poetry of the Deaf
Archibald Macleish | Ars Poetica | 8
Willard Madsen | You Have to be Deaf to Understand | 9
Willard Madsen | No | 11
David Wright | Monologue of a Deaf Man | 13
David Wright | By the Effigy of Saint Cecilia | 15
Joachim de Bellay | Hyme a la Surdité | 16
Agatha Tiegel | Semi–Mutes | 17
Maria Okwara | Silence | 18
Mervin Garretson | Flight 137: the Reality of Deafness | 20
Robert Panara | On His Deafness | 21
Robert Panara | Poetry and Deaf Culture | 22
Deaf Children
Elizabeth Ward | My Welcome to your World of Silence | 32
Mervin Garretson | Words from a Deaf Child | 33
Jennifer Kelsall | Maternity Care for the Deaf: a living concern | 34
Agatha Tiegel | Lottie Anderson | 36
George Montgomery | A Cup of Kindness | 37
Deaf History and Culture
Jack Gannon | Of Roots and Wings...and the Family of Man | 41
Robert Grieve | Isolation Experiments on Children's Language | 46
Armin Löwe | Errare Humanum Est | 53
Arthur Dimmock | The Essence of Tommy | 64
Charles Sheriff | On Seeing Garrick Act | 67
Willard Madsen | My Rainbow, My World | 68
Aaron Williamson | A Holythroat Symposium | 69
Academic & Media Language
Mervin Garretson | for Bill Stokoe | 74
Willard Madsen | At the Beach | 75
Murray Holmes | Language for the Brain | 76
Helen Reed | The Academic Muse: Academic Writing for Deaf Students | 83
George Montgomery | Academic Writing: Varieties of English for Students | 85
Chris Brand | Some Advice on Essay Writing for Undergraduate Students | 94
Bob Duncan | Bias and Balance in Television Writing for Deaf Viewers | 98
Charles Donaldson | Over the Wall | 103
George Montgomery | The Vicar of Braidwood | 106
Publication and Politics
Agatha Tiegel | The Intellect of Women | 110
Halla Beloff | Up for PC or Down with Sexism | 112
Raymond Lee | The Onset of Deaf Liberation | 115
George Montgomery | The Deaf Samizdat | 119
Elizabeth Mapstone | Communicating Specialist Knowledge | 125
Kenneth Jones | Editing "Deafness" | 130
Mervin Garretson | Diversity and Solidarity in the Deaf Perspective | 132
Pauline Jordan | Face to Face with John Hay | 134
Gordon Davidson | A Background to Production | 139
George Montgomery | Jabberwocky and Jargonese | 141

Bibiliography | | 165
Epilogue
George Montgomery | Hail and Farewell | 168
Bilbo Monaghan | Time | 170
Index | | 171

PROLOGUE

"The word becomes the picture
in this language for the eye."

We
Loved your
Gentle   ways
And cannot even now
Begin   to   face   our   loss
Until   our   pain   grows   less.
So we took these roughhewn words
and shaped them as a cairn in tribute,
On your native hills where we can always climb
And stay to add a stone and share a sign with you.

Introduction: Publishing and the Deaf

by

George Montgomery and Gordon Davidson

On 29 August 1992 a small group of deaf intellectuals addressed a Scottish Workshop seminar of 26, mostly profoundly deaf people in Strathclyde Regional Headquarters, Glasgow.

It was interesting because, whilst most papers were given in British Sign Language, they were about Deaf literature in English. The introductory paper was about deaf people training in publications and was given by Gordon Davidson and Anne Cumming with a voice over by George Montgomery. It explained how difficult it is for deaf writers to get their books published and how in many areas deaf workers are not allowed into printing work or into the printing unions. To stop this discrimination the Scottish Workshop set up its own press in Donaldson's College which itself was founded by a wealthy Edinburgh printer, James Donaldson, who left all his money to the great benefit of generations of deaf people. Now SWP produces books written by Deaf authors, about Deaf people, community and concerns and printed by Deaf typesetters, layout specialists and marketed by deaf staff and trainees, guided by Deaf instructors.

The next paper by A F Dimmock, a noted author and BDA gold medallist told the story of his biography of the famous Royal Artist and member of the Royal Academy, "Tommy" Thomson. This was an inspiring story of a man who refused the "Deaf-can't" advice of parents and teachers and in a tempestuous life of struggle and genius, showed the world, "Deaf-can". What a shame more deaf people and workers with the deaf do not read this and Mr Dimmock's other great contributions to Deaf culture, his illustrated history of Deaf Sport in his "Sporting Heritage" printed by Victor Boni and Cruel Legacy, an introduction to the record of deaf people in history.

After this Raymond Lee of the London NUD, gave a gripping account of the editing and collection of papers written on the theme of "Deaf Liberation". This followed the story from the "dark ages" of pure oralism, through the struggle for Total Communication and for recognition of deaf culture to the television-friendly, relatively liberated present day. Mr Lee recorded the initial official hostility to the idea of a healthy, robust Deaf culture by the kind of people who are now eager to jump on the BSL gravy train now that it is safe to do so.

The next speaker, Jennifer Kelsall, Midwifery Team Leader, Wythenshawe Hospital began by showing a film with signs and sub-titles. It was about the special problems deaf mothers face before, after and during the process of giving birth to a baby. Her book "Maternity Care for the Deaf" printed by SWP was itself brought into the world at this seminar. Mrs Kelsall proved to be a real credit to her profession, showing a total dedication to this specialist part of midwifery. Because of her restless round of attendance at births, training midwives and arranging workshops and deaf birth awareness courses – for deaf and hearing – we will all benefit from her work and should see more of her in the future; we certainly hope so. Her inclusion in this volume reminds us of the need for clear, accurate English in Science where poetic elaboration is a dangerous luxury.

All in all, the participants learnt a lot and had a good time even before the discussion under the direction of Chairmen M Holmes and J Hay moved to the Bon Accord off Sauchiehall Street. They departed back to Scotland, Ireland, Denmark, Shetland and England with a final note of appreciation to our host Alex McPherson, Regional Coordinator of Deaf Services and to the hospitable citizens of the Ancient Kingdom/People's Republic of Strathclyde.

We published the original seminar proceedings along with a few papers from people unable to attend in person. From this beginning, the importance of deaf writing became more obvious to us and, as we began collecting more and more examples of this, the present book took shape.

We were about to send it to the binders on two occasions when events overtook us and additions seemed advisable. The first time was when Arthur Dimmock's exciting new book "The Cruel Legacy" had to be printed and the second occasion was the sad loss of a pioneer deaf writer, dramatist and poet, when Dot Miles died in early 1993.

Delays and the ever-receding deadline turned out to be beneficial as in this time overseas writers of the calibre of David Wright in Portugal, Bob Panara and Merv Garretson in USA expressed their willingness to contribute. Some less established newcomers to Deaf poetry also volunteered their work, giving us the though provoking, contrast between the introspective semantic rumination of Maria Okwara and the identity bashing, phatic spate of Aaron Williamson, pounding out his soul to the beat of the bodhran (Gaelic for deaf drum). Given the recent upsurge of interest in the history of Deaf people, the paper by Bob Grieve on early attempts at "experimental" artificial speech deprivation is included for its intrinsic interest but also as an example of how careful scholarship can give an accurate record of traditions which have hitherto echoed vaguely throughout the literature on deafness like the uncertain hearsay of Russian scandal. A more consciously direct attack on historical inaccuracy is the devastating intellectual honesty of Armin Löwe who reminds us bluntly that appropriate as it may be to literature the "willing suspension of disbelief" has no place whatsoever in historical works. The papers on the current use of English had one obvious omission which Halla Beloff generously volunteered to cover in her account of the recent move away from language which imparts a sexist bias from the author to his/her reader. Finally, in 1994, the editor George Montgomery was appointed to the Powrie Vaux Doctor Chair of Deaf Studies in Gallaudet University and was thus enabled to make new relationships with deaf writers and to renew old ties with Jack Gannon, most popular writer of Deaf history and with Will Madsen, that unassuming writer of the best known poems on deafness ever produced. The Gallaudet contact is also evident in the evocatively appropriate lines from Bilbo Monaghan who died in February 1994.

The resulting anthology is an unusual mixture which combines examples of deaf writing with papers about the conditions of writing and publishing the deaf view with background information about the use and importance of English in Deaf Literature. As with many anthologies, the variety and contrast is important for readers who may wish to dip into the pages in desultory fashion to ruminate on the verdant literary fodder within. For the more systematic reader, a light structure of subject areas has been outlined in the contents page. Chapters, however, do not easily fit the labels and are more realistically seen as arranged along a spectrum, gradually changing from the poetical to the more prosaic world of politics, publishing and technicalities.

Poetry and literature are rarely cost-effective, especially with the minuscule market in the Deaf community. Thus, most of the considerable work put into this volume is voluntary and the observable gusto in contributions confirms that the enjoyment of expression is in itself a reward. We hope readers may share some of this enjoyment and that it helps to escape a life of cost-effective misery devoid of poetry.

Acknowledgements are gratefully recorded to:-

Carcanet Press, Creations Books, NAD Monographs, BPS, BDA, NUD, British Journal of

Teachers of the Deaf, Scottish Workshop Publications and to the executor of Dorothy Miles for permission to publish individual items.

More immediate thanks are due to Colin White and Susan Napier of Donaldson's College for their wholehearted production of typescript and graphics. Mrs Napier herself gave the definitive compliment to the contribution of Agatha Tiegel Hanson when she returned the completed script with a query about the 1893 date: "Should this not be 1993?" she asked, as the script reads as if it were written last year not last century.

A Deaf Poetess

Dorothy May Squire Miles 1931–1993
by
Donald E Read

Dorothy or Dot, as she was more widely known, was born in the village of Gwernaffield near Mold in North Wales. Moving to Rhyl soon after, she attended Christ Church Elementary School Rhyl and there took part in school plays and also the local dramatic society with the rest of her family. They spent many a happy day watching the Summer shows at the Open Air Amphitheatre on the prom. Dorothy, who could read at the age of 3, was introduced to poetry by her sister Jean, 10 years older, who passed on to her the love of poetry, particularly romantic poetry.

Meningitis struck in 1940 and left her completely deaf resulting in her being sent to the Royal Schools for the Deaf, Old Trafford, Manchester. Here, as 152, she was soon in demand after school for her famous story-telling in sign, which set her on the road to Deaf Theatre and Poems in Sign. From 1946–1950, she attended Mary Hare Grammar School where she wrote the poems "Cloud Magic" and "On the Downs" before starting work in a number of jobs including her first job with the Road Research Laboratory when she wrote "Exaltation", then Liverpool Benevolent Society for the Aid of the Deaf and Dumb when she wrote "Dawn from the River".

Moving to America, she attended Gallaudet College, Washington, USA 1957–1961 to get her BA in English and winning the best Actress award and had Poetry and Prose published in "The Silent Muse" in 1960, then on to Howard University to do an incomplete MA in Sociology. This was followed by a number of jobs in the USA before attending the Connecticut College with the National Theatre Institute where she took her MA in Educational Theatre: thesis; "A History of Theatre in the Deaf Community of the United States."

Joining the National Theatre of the Deaf, she took part in many productions and took on practically most jobs needed in running a successful production. From 1970–1973, she was Editor and Columnist for NTD Spotlight and she wrote what is possibly her best known poem "Seasons" (an exercise in Haiku) in 1970.

1973 saw her write "A Play of our Own", an Original play in three scenes about deaf people which has been very successful on both sides of the Atlantic. Dorothy not only wrote it she had also directed and acted in it as circumstances required.

"Gestures" poetry in Sign Language was published in 1973 in America and contains all herpoems written before 1973, fifteen of the poems signed by Dorothy were filmed and sold in film and video tape form throughout America.

On returning to England in 1977, she worked as a social worker in Uxbridge, then research worker in Sign Language for the BDA in Newcastle where I met her. There she soon introduced us to the beauty of her sign poetry taking the opportunity at workshops and gatherings to charm us with what, to us at that time, was something unknown and incredibly beautiful. She wrote many more poems in England and some she performed in private and in public. The commencement of Deaf Television Programmes introduced many other deaf people to her poetry for the first time.

It has been a privilege as her close friend for all the years since her return from American to be able to see at first hand many of her new poems before anyone else as she was forever striving for perfection and would try new poems on me over and over again before she was satisfied that they were what she wanted to express.

Apart from the theatre and poetry, Dorothy loved to sign the songs from the musicals. It never took much to set Dorothy off – a thought, a picture, a chance word from someone and she would launch into a lively rendering from a Gilbert and Sullivan play no matter where she was or who she was with: this could be disturbing for some people. Her repertoire was as wide and as varied as anyone could imagine – how she could remember all those songs and be word perfect every time was truly remarkable. I shall always cherish the sight of her signing a duet with her lifelong friend Charles Herd at some Deaf gathering or other. Reciting other poets' work activated her truly remarkable empathy and memory.

It was always uppermost in Dorothy's mind that others should be able to share in the beauty and pleasure that sign poetry gave to her with the result that she gave signed poetry and creative sign workshops around the country in the hope that others could be able to follow her lead.

"I think that I shall never see, a poem lovely as a tree" wrote Mary Shelley but, through Dorothy, I came to doubt this view and to accept both as expressions of beauty without conflict. I was able to share my lifelong love of trees with her, though she already loved trees and had written about them in "Exaltation". I was able, through my work as Forester, to give her a closer insight and knowledge of them which led to many walks in Jesmond Dene at Newcastle and Regent's Park in London and other places looking at and admiring the trees. This would more often than not lead to her bubbling over with poetry and song in praise of nature; "Then, for a moment, from this lowly sod I reached with them to touch the face of God".

Language for the Eye

by
Dorothy Miles

Hold a tree in the palm of your hand,
or topple it with a crash,
Sail a boat on finger waves,
or sink it with a splash.
From your finger tips see a frog leap,
at a passing butterfly.
The word becomes the picture in this language for the eye.

Follow the sun from rise to set,
or bounce it like a ball.
Catch a fish in a fishing net,
or swallow it, bones and all.
Make traffic scurry, or airplanes fly,
and people meet and part.
The word becomes the action in this language of the heart.

POETRY OF THE
DEAF

**"Poetry is a sword of lightning
forever unsheathed
Which consumes the scabbard that
would contain it"**

P.B. Shelley

Ars Poetica

by
Archibald Macleish – 1926

A poem should be palpable and mute
As a globed fruit,
Dumb
As old medallions to the thumb,
Silent as the sleeve-worn stone
Of casement ledges where the moss has grown--
A poem should be wordless
As the flight of birds.
A poem should be motionless in time
As the moon climbs,
Leaving, as the moon releases
Twig by twig the night-entangled trees,
Leaving, as the moon behind the winter leaves,
Memory by memory the mind--
A poem should be motionless in time
As the moon climbs.
A poem should be equal to:
Not true.
For all the history or grief
An empty doorway and a maple leaf.
For love
The leaning grasses and two lights above the sea--
A poem should not mean
But be.

You Have to be Deaf to Understand
by
Willard J Madsen

What is it like "hear" a hand?
You have to be deaf to understand!

What is it like to be a small child,
In a school, in a room void of sound –
With a teacher who talks and talks and talks;
And then when she does come around to you,
She expects you to know what she's said?
You have to be deaf to understand.

Or the teacher who thinks that to make you smart,
You must first learn how to talk with your voice;
So mumbo-jumbo with hands on your face
For hours and hours without patience or end,
Until out comes a faint resembling sound?
You have to be deaf to understand.

What is it like to be curious,
To thirst for knowledge you can call your own,
With an inner desire that's set on fire –
And you ask a brother, sister, or friend
Who looks in answer and says, "Never mind!"?
You have to be deaf to understand.

What is it like in a corner to stand,
Though there's nothing you've done really wrong,
Other than try to make use of your hands
To a silent peer to communicate
A thought that comes to your mind all at once?
You have to be deaf to understand.

What is it like to be shouted at
When one thinks that will help you to hear;
Or misunderstand the words of a friend
Who is trying to make a joke clear,
And you don't get the point because he's failed?
You have to be deaf to understand.

What is it like to be laughed in the face
When you try to repeat what is said;
Just to make sure that you've understood,
And you find that the words were misread –

9

And you want to cry out, "Please help me, friend!"?
You have to be deaf to understand.

What is it like to have to depend
Upon one who can hear to phone a friend;
Or place a call to a business firm
And be forced to share what's personal, and,
Then find that your message wasn't made clear?
You have to be deaf to understand.

What is it like to be deaf and alone
In the company of those who can hear –
And you only guess as you go along,
For no one's there with a helping hand,
As you try to keep up with words and song?
You have to be deaf to understand.

What is it like on the road of life
To meet with a stranger who opens his mouth –
And speaks out a line at a rapid pace;
And you can't understand the look on his face
Because it is new and you're lost in the race?
You have to be deaf to understand.

What is it like to comprehend
Some nimble fingers that paint the scene,
And make you smile and feel serene
With the "spoken word" of the moving hand
That makes you part of the world at large?
You have to be deaf to understand.

What is it like to "hear" a hand?
Yes, you have to be deaf to understand!

NO
by
Willard Madsen

I'm tired of hearing
That old refrain:
"Teach the deaf to speak – to talk
And they'll be whole again!"

How well I know
That's just not so!
I live; I grow
And everyday
Quite simply tells me:
"NO!"

I'm deaf –
I cannot hear.
And I know –
No magic will
Ever transform me
Into being otherwise!

I talk.
You smile;
You understand
My simple message spoken.
"Bravo!"
"What marvellous speech!"

You pat me on the back and say:
"It's a hearing world you must live in
Or be quite simply,
Relegated to
A stigmatized
Deaf ghetto ghetto ghetto ghetto
A world of silence:
A world of signs:
A limited world
Apart from the rest!"

NO!
That's not the world at all:
Not the world I know:
My world is
Beautiful
Unlimited
Not perfect, but
Neither void:

How can it be
When all around me
Are
Hands
Faces,
Whole beings
Communicating?
And I understand all that's said;
No guessing,
Doubting,
Struggling,
To fill in the gaps –
Words unrecognised or missed!

You praise my speech:
My comprehension
That's fine, but ...
You soon forget
Frustrations endured ...
The difficulties faced!
I cannot be like you.
NO!
We're set apart ...
But only by one small difference –
A difference at times
That overwhelms:
I do not hear;
I cannot hear!

Yes! Teach the deaf
To speak – to talk,
But teach them first
How to walk
With confidence,
With heads held high,
And full knowledge
To converse by
With "words" flowing from the hand!

Let them carry
Throughout this land
A simple banner
Called "Self–Esteem",
And teach the world at large to sign –
To make us all
One world at heart
And not a world
That's set apart!
NO!

Monologue of a Deaf Man
by
David Wright
"Et lui comprit trop bien, n'ayant pas entendu"
Tristan Corbière

It is a good plan, and began with childhood
As my fortune discovered, only to hear
How much it is necessary to have said.
Oh silence, independent of a stopped ear,
You observe birds, flying, sing with wings instead.

Then do you console yourself? You are consoled
If you are, as all are. So easy a youth
Still unconcerned with the concern of a world
Where, masked and legible, a moment of truth
Manifests what, gagged, a tongue should have told;

Still observer of vanity and courage
And of these mirror as well; that is something
More than a sound of violin to assuage
What the human being most dies of: boredom
Which makes hedgebirds clamour in their blackthorn cage.

But did the brushless fox die of eloquence?
No, but talked himself, it seems, into a tale.
The injury, dominated, is an asset:
It is there for domination, that is all.
Else what must faith do deserted by mountains?

Talk to me then, you who have so much to say,
Spectator of the human conversation,
Reader of tongues, examiner of the eye,
And detective of clues in every action,
What could a voice, if you heard it, signify?

The tone speaks less than a twitch and a grimace.
People make to depart, do not say 'Goodbye.'
Decision, indecision, drawn on every face
As if they spoke. But what do they really say?
You are not spared, either, the banalites.

In whatever condition, whole, blind, dumb,
Onelegged or leprous, the human being is,
I affirm the human condition is the same,
The heart half broken in ashes and in lies,
But sustained by the immensity of the divine.

Thus I too must praise out of a quiet ear
The great creation to which I owe I am
My grief and my love. O hear me if I cry
Among the din of birds deaf to their acclaim,
Involved like them in the not unhearing air.

By the Effigy of Saint Cecilia
by
David Wright

Having peculiar reverence for this creature
Of the numinous imagination, I am come
To visit her church and stand before the altar
Where her image, hewn in pathetic stone,
Exhibits the handiwork of her executioner.

There are the axemarks. Outside, in the courtyard,
In shabby habit, an Italian nun
Came up and spoke: I had to answer, 'Sordo.'
She said she was a teacher of deaf children
And had experience of my disorder.

And I have had experience of her order,
Interpenetrating chords and marshalled sound;
Often I loved to listen to the organ's
Harmonious and concordant interpretation
Of what is due from us to the creation.

But it was taken from me in my childhood
And those graduated pipes turned into stone.
Now, having travelled a long way through silence,
Within the church in Trastevere I stand
A pilgrim to the patron saint of music.

And am abashed by the presence of this nun
Beside the embodiment of that legendary
Virgin whose music and whose martyrdom
Is special to this place: by her reality.
She is a reminder of practical kindness.

The care it takes to draw speech from the dumb
Or pierce with sense the carapace of deafness;
And so, of the plain humility of the ethos
That constructed, also, this elaborate room
To pray for bread in; they are not contradictory.

Lines from Hyme à la Surdité

by Joachim du Bellay
translated by David Wright

All that I have of good, that in myself I value,
Is to be without shame and without pretence, like you;
To prove a good comrade, and to keep good faith,
And to be, dear Ronsard, like you, half deaf:
Half deaf! What a fortune! Would to God I had had
Enough good luck to be deaf as an egg.
I am not one of those whose inflated poetry
Will create a mastodon out of a small fly,
But without altering a white to a black colour,
Or pretending a happiness to hide a dolour,
I will say that to be deaf – for those who know
The difference between good and evil (they are few) –
Is not an evil, only seems to be so.

NB   This poem was written for Pierre Ronsard who became deaf after a
shipwreck whilst escorting Mary Stuart from France to be crowned
Queen of Scots.

Note the use of the term "half-deaf" derived from the
pejorative sign used by deaf people to denote partial deafness
in the manner of the racist term "half-breed".

Semi-Mutes
by
Agatha Tiegel – 1892

A river deep of silence
E'er swells our souls around.
It's tide flows and submerges
The weaker tide of sound.

Now memory flashes through us,
Now lingers with us long.
Sweet strains of vanished music
Make up its haunting song.

Yet must we bear our burden.
Yet must we walk our way,
And slowly, surely build a work
That will endure for aye.

We can control the future,
Can live for well or ill
Let us clasp hands and forward.
There is no standing still.

Silence
by
Maria Grace Okwara – 1992

Awakening

On a sunny morning
Back in seventy-four
I awoke up in my bed
Changed forever.

Took me a while
To identify the change
When screaming began
All was silent to me.

It took a scolding
From someone beloved
To make me realize
I would be deaf forever.

Realisation

A wall of silence
Surrounds me.
Is it for protection,
or a barrier?

Silence
What are its benefits?
Peace of Mind
And solitude.

As one can see,
Silence has multi-meanings
It can be good or bad
And oftentimes it's golden.

I can not hear
But through my mind
There's a cacophony of sounds
That are now lost to me.

Yet, I do not mind
For I have Learned to
Appreciate the use of my eyes
And the dance of hands.

Re-awakening

If you knew
What I feel,

If you knew
The color and radiance of the sun.

If you could smell the flowers
And notice the shape of their petals.

If you could read a smile or a frown
In a loved one's face.

If you could see
The shape, texture, and posture of things.

You would not say
I live in "silence"

Flight 137
the reality of deafness
by
Mervin Garretson

my reality against your pretense
your truths may not be mine
I'm not you you're not me
take a garden crowned with flowers
some are roses some are not
take a basket filled with fruit
some are peaches some are not.

take a heaven filled with clouds
some are cirrus some are not
take a cellar stocked with wine
some is vintage some is not.

take a classroom filled with love
some are hearing some are not
some are knowing some are not
some are tender some are true.

some are for some are with
some are a some are the
some mean well some know better
some can speak and some cannot.

some know books some know life
some have faith some have doubt
some know what it's all about
some have eyes but cannot see
some have hearing but are deaf
these are deafer than the deaf.

On His Deafness

by
Robert F Panara

My ears are deaf, and yet I seem to hear
Sweet nature's music and the songs of man
For I have learned from Fancy's artisan
How written words can thrill the inner ear
Just as they move the heart, and so for me
They also seem to ring out loud and free.

In silent study I have learned to tell
Each secret shade of meaning and to hear
A magic harmony, at once sincere,
That somehow notes the tinkle of a bell,
The cooing of a dove, the swish of leaves,
The raindrop's pitter-patter on the eaves,
The lover's sigh, the thrumming of guitar,
And, if I choose, the rustle of a star!

Poetry and Deaf Culture

by
Robert Panara

What is Poetry? Is it something whose secrets are known only to a certain group of people, or is it that something which may be cultivated and developed to suit the taste and fancy of everyone? Is poetry an art, or is it a science? Is it difficult to learn, or is it easy to master? And, as to the relative value of the subject itself, is it of any importance to learn poetry, or is it of no consequence at all in this modern day and age? The answers to each of these questions will be dealt with privately, not with regard to the ears of the hearing but to those of our own kind – the ears that hear no sound.

It is my belief that poetry has as great a proportion of followers among deaf people as it has among the hearing. The reason for this is simple. The deaf are not a bit different than their hearing brethren, despite the fact that a great many people believe otherwise. Simply because we cannot hear does not mean that our hearts are locked to the twin qualities of sentiment and emotion. Poetry, unlike music, is made up of words, and as long as the deaf are able to read and to understand the meaning of these words they will learn to love poetry and the wisdom, the beauty, the rhythm and the music that are found therein.

One may wonder how it is possible for the deaf to learn rhythm and music. Let me attempt to explain. Music, that is, the interpretation made popular with most people, concerns those sounds which are caused to emanate from material implements constructed by man. These are our musical instruments, and we call them by such names as "the violin, the flute, and the piano," to mention a few. We believe that they can be made to imitate the chirping of birds, the roaring of winds, and the moaning of the sea. Many are of the opinion that it is impossible for the deaf to hear these sounds merely by reading the word symbol which stands for their equivalent, and few people can understand how the deaf are able to enjoy poems that deal with and emphasize such sounds. This is where they are mistaken. The deaf cannot hear them, but they can imagine each of the sounds. And if they can imagine the peculiar moaning of sound made by the sea, isn't it likely that they may also feel the same way as other people feel when they hear these sounds?

As an illustration, let me offer the following example. Suppose a deaf person were to read the following lines from Matthew Arnold's poem, "Dover Beach":–

> *"Listen"! you hear the grating roar*
> *Of pebbles which the waves draw back, and fling,*
> *At their return up the high strand,*
> *Begin, and cease, and then again begin,*
> *With tremulous cadence of slow, and bring*
> *The eternal note of sadness in...."*

As long as this person understood the meaning of the words, "grating" and "roar", and provided that he had seen, either in actuality or in pictures, the rise and fall of the waves splashing upon a sandy shore, this person would be able to imagine the noise made. He could sense "the grating roar" that sounded when the breakers smashed down upon the pebbly beach and ground the tiny particles together. He could picture the monotonous ebb and flow of the waters and paint with his imagination the "tremulous cadence slow" of the whole scene, until he actually felt the note of sadness which crept into the poet's mood. In short, he hears by reading and digesting the words of the poem and by letting his imagination connect every symbol of sound together until there is formed an expressive music.

By this same process, the deafened person also experiences that quality which we call, "rhythm." His knowledge of how the waves rise and fall in measured timing, and the picture which the words of the poem draw up for him are sufficient to arouse the sense of rhythm which highlights the poet's interpretation. The awareness of rhythm and timing is not alien to the soul of the deafened person. He has it when he feels the rhythmatic throbbing of a printing press in operation; he is conscious of it when watching an eight-oared racing crew in action, or when he thrills to the precision-like grace of a corps of ballet dancers; and he experiences the same sensation when pedalling on his bicycle, when punching at the keys of his typewriter, when chopping the wood for his winter fuel. What does it matter if he cannot hear the rhythm of beautiful music? His remaining senses are yet alive and vibrant to the rhythm of movement, to the touch of timing. He does not need to hear music in order to comprehend rhythm. He experiences it in his daily life, and it is this quality which makes him both understand and feel the rhythm in poetry.

It is no secret that man, throughout the ages, has forever been trying to set down in writing the things he has seen, and heard, or otherwise sensed in the world about him. Whatever was pleasing to the ear, he has put down in the language of music, and that which appealed more to the eye, he has written in the language of poetry. Of these two forms of self-expression, the language of poetry is the one which is composed solely of words. And because it is composed of words, poetry requires a reader who will make the effort of reading in order to experience the sentiment and the emotion which are pent up within these words. His position is unique because he has to depend entirely upon himself as a means of enjoying the poem of his choice, whereas the music lover has only to go the opera house, or tune in his radio, or play his favorite gramophone record, and his enjoyment will be complete.

Poetry and music have been linked together as being the twin sisters of all the arts. Yet, we find a greater number of people who are more interested in listening to music than in reading poetry. This is not surprising. Music is the universal language of all people. Its interpretation is the same to all ears, and it awakens the same kindred passions in the blood of any nationality of a people. Unlike poetry, one does not have to read in order to understand music, and it is much easier to sit back comfortably and let the strains of a beautiful song flow into one's ears and fill the soul with happiness than to take in hand a book of poems and labor over the diction of a peculiar language in order to experience the same feeling.

This is the exact point where the deafened person fits into the picture. Because of the fact that their ears are locked to music, it is only natural that the deaf should turn to poetry as a means of consolation. If they were trained rightly in the schoolroom, and granted that they possess a good command of language, there is every reason to encourage the deaf to read a great deal of poetry. They may gain as much enjoyment as other people who can hear may derive from music. Their senses can be trained to welcome the thousand and one pulsating passions of the heart and soul which rise from the thrill of living. In it they will hear the song of the skylark, the whisper of the night-wind, the laughter of the rippling brook, the clamor of a great city at work. They will find deep peace and happiness in listening to "The Psalms of David," and they will be fired with the love of patriotism when they thrill to the fife and drum beat of Kipling's stirring ballads. They will sense the sinister silence made manifest by Poe's brooding "Raven," and they will shrink and shudder at every eerie tolling of "The Bells."

And poetry can be of aid to the deaf in yet another way. Its pleasing rhyme and rhythm may teach them to balance their writing style so that theirs may more nearly resemble the form of a hearing person's. Although we deaf cannot hear the way a sweet-sounding and well-balanced sentence would be written down, nevertheless, we may be trained to develop a certain smoothness and a fine sense of timing with our words by studying the harmonious and rhythmic speech of poetry. For poetry is both an art and a science, just like the subject of English. It is composed of grammar as well as of composition. From its syntax, we learn the rhyme, the rhythm, the scientific structure of the whole, and from its artistry we develop a taste and discrimination for using only those words which can best illustrate what we want to say – the very same words over which the poet labors so diligently to order to find the right expression for his thoughts. Despite this, we still find unimaginative teachers of the language arts who avoid poems and, have enough problems, it seems, with improving the communication skills of deaf students through reading and writing. Why, indeed, run the risk of having students develop negative attitudes toward the study of literature, such as by exposing them to the language of metaphor and abstract ideas? Moreover, isn't it unrealistic to expect deaf students to respond to special sound effects of poetic expression?

Why teach poetry? For the very same reason that we teach the language arts. Poetry is one of the best means of developing concepts of ideas, enlarging a vocabulary and improving overall skills. It helps stimulate creativity and self expression, and it encourages the development of a student's intellectual faculties – imagination, thinking, and interpretation. Finally, as in exposure to dramatics or dancing, it makes students react emotionally and sensitively to artistry of expression. If this be paradox, it is no more startling than the truth of a poem, "Blind," by Harry Kemp:

> The Spring blew trumpets of color;
> Her Green sang in my brain...
> I heard a blind man groping
> "Tap-Tap" with his cane.
>
> I pitied him in his blindness,
> But can I boast, "I see"?
> Perhaps there walks a spirit
> Close by, who pities me –
>
> A spirit who hears me tapping
> the five sensed cane of mind
> Amid such unguessed glories –
> That I–am worse than blind!

It has often been said that it is a waste of time and energy to teach poetry to deaf persons because of their inability to respond to the connotation of words, to figurative language, and to the artistic use of sound. Ironically, these linguistic skills are just what the deaf have need to learn if we hope to see them attain a certain mastery of reading and develop sophistication in communication and expression. The study of poetry can help the deaf person develop a sharpened sensitivity to language and show him how words are given rich and precise meaning through their association and interrelations with other words.

Poetry deals with words and with the arrangement of words in a special way so as to enhance their meaning and their total impression upon the senses. Where deaf persons are concerned, it is not enough for them to learn the literal meaning of words. Deaf persons need to discover the suggestive power of words that can enrich their understanding of the various shades and tones and moods which give individuality to persons, places, and things. Poetry also provides a rich store of multi-sensory images for the deaf person laboring to relate the raw material of his life experiences to the illimitable experiences of the creative imagination. As Shakespeare so eloquently phrased it:

> *"The Poet's eye, in a fine frenzy rolling,*
> *Doth glance from heaven to earth, from earth to heaven;*
> *And as imagination bodies forth*
> *The forms of things unknown, the poet's pen*
> *Turns them to shapes and gives to airy nothing*
> *A local habitation and a name."*

Through the language of poetry, students can learn to perceive how the commonplace is made to seem uncommon, how old words can be expressed with freshness, originality, and beauty. It takes imagination to see reality, and the language of poetry has an ingenious way of bringing this about. One of these ways is by method of simile and metaphor, in which a comparison is made of two things seemingly unlike or unrelated. Take, for example, the following:

> *"The river is a snake which coils on itself."*

All of us know, only too well, that most deaf persons tend to develop fixed views of the universe and of life. Thus, rivers are usually described as either "winding" or "curving" when not flowing in straight lines, and hardly any deaf student would ever think of relating snakes to rivers, except for the kind which make their habitat therein. But here is a river "which coils on itself" like a snake! The comparison is not only fresh and startling; it is also quite real to the experience of the deaf student. Better still, he now discovers how his own vicarious experiences can be given meaningful relationships. Gradually, too, he learns how new dimensions can be given to words, building up his word power and expressive skills. Thus, a verb form such as "coils on itself" can expand his vocabulary and help him to attain the more abstract reaches of language.

The experienced teacher can quickly exploit this new found interest and discovery by relating it to other descriptive examples. His anthology of poetic metaphors can quickly range from Kipling's snake which "poured itself along the ground" to Emily Dickinson's "Narrow Fellow In The Grass" which, suddenly, "wrinkled and was gone!"

Similarly, by recalling the experiences with nature, the student can be taught to appreciate such picturesque images as "blackbirds peppering the sky," "poppies nodding like red coals" and "radiant raindrops couching in cool flowers."

From here, too, it might prove a meaningful transition to guide the student's interest toward the understanding and appreciation of the poetic uses of alliteration. By relating the lessons learned in speech and speechreading class, he can be made to perceive that the same words which so vividly describe a thing or an action can also provide multi-sensory impressions that, taken together, can yield greater extension of meaning. The following lines from Keats' "Ode To A Nightingale" may demonstrate this feature:

> *"O for a beaker full of the warm South,*
> *Full of the true, the blushful Hippocrene,*
> *With beaded bubbles winking at the brim,*
> *And purple-stained mouth"*

The alliterative repetition of certain syllables in these lines evokes an empathetic response in the deaf person reading them aloud or while reading the teacher's lips. The plosive "b" and "p" sounds of "beaker", "blushful", "beaded bubbles", "brim" and "purple", coupled with the fricative "f" sounds of "full", will actually get the deaf person to see the tempting cup of brew, filled to overflowing,

"With beaded bubbles winking at the brim"

and simultaneously sense the warmth, the fullness, the ripening splendor of the Southland from whence it originated. Indeed, he can actually smack his lips in anticipation of quaffing such a rare vintage wine from a beaker that will leave a purple stain around the mouth and fill him with exuberance of bountiful health and happiness.

Not only does poetry stimulate the imagination and build word power but it is also ideally suited to developing skills in reading comprehension and written expression. Reading comes before writing. In order to write well, one must first be able to read with complete understanding. One must perceive how writers express their every thought and observation with precision, how they organize language to convey the exact meanings intended.

Poetry suits this purpose neatly. Its brevity fits the needs of the classroom lesson in the language arts, usually lasting for an hour. This does not hold true of all poems, of course. The teacher will have to give much advance planning to the selection of poems which contain a minimum of hard words, inverted sentences, and elliptic constructions. The ideal poem would thus contain words and phrases that are mostly familiar to the student at his or her particular grade level; its syntax would correspond with the normal word order of prose; and it would be comparatively short. Thus, the student would always have sight of the whole while analyzing each of its parts. Such a poem, moreover, could easily be strung out on the chalkboard, if desired, and written as prose. This might offer opportunity to teach grammar and word usage based on actual models of literature.

For purposes of illustration, let us briefly study the following translations from the Japanese haikus:

> *Umbrella*
> *As I walk in the winter rain,*
> *The umbrella*
> *Pushes me back.*
>
> *(Shisei–Jo)*

Deaf students might profitably be asked to imitate the action of the speaker in the poem, holding an imaginary umbrella in hand. On the first try, most of them will undoubtedly end up stumbling backwards, holding the umbrella at a sharp angle behind the shoulder to indicate how it is pulling them back. But is the umbrella pulling you back? Study the poem again!

After further study and comment, the students will grasp the idea that the wind is pushing hard against the hood of the umbrella and that the only possible way of holding on to it is by pointing it into the very face of the wind. What kind of wind is it? What does the poem say to suggest this?" "It must be a strong wind, of course," observes one student. "Ah I know!" chimes in another, "It's a winter rain!" It is winter in Japan; it is raining and the wind is blowing very hard – like a strong March wind in our country!"

> *As I walk in the winter rain, the umbrella*
> *pushes me back.*

Let us now take the following poem to see how figures of speech are often meaningfully related to the poetic sound structure:

Hail
In the abandoned boat
The hail
Bounces about.

> *(Shiki)*

After careful study and discussion, the teacher should be able to make the deaf students realize why the hail is "bouncing about." Suddenly, by cupping both hands together, they will visualize the shape of the boat and perceive that it determines how the ricocheting hail bounces about. Just as suddenly, they will become aware of the fact that the boat is abandoned. Nobody is in the boat and the hail is bouncing about merrily, having a good time. Once this mood is established and the class is in boisterous spirits, mimicking the bouncing about of the hailstones in the boat, it will prove a nice surprise to learn how the alliteration of certain syllables imitates the sound effects of the action.

Listen to the plosive "b" of abandoned, boat, bounces, about! Feel your cheeks blowing up and let your lips burst out the "b" sounds! Think of the word "bombardment" – you know, the bombardment of cannons, when the guns of war are booming, when they bombard the walls of a fortress with bursting bombs!

"That's what is happening in the boat!" exclaims one excited student, "the boat is being bombarded by hail!" "No!" argues another student, "the sound is softer than that. It's more like a bump, bump, bumpety–bump of bouncing pebbles!" "Yes!" choruses the whole class. "It's a merry sound because the hail is having a good time in the abandoned boat!"

> *In the abandoned boat, the hail bounces about.*

Such figurative uses of language are sure to motivate students to observe details which they have never noticed before. Additionally, they will soon become aware of how the imagery of poetry can impress itself upon their sensibilities. Let us take a third poem to see how this works in still other ways:

The Barley Field
Up the barley rows,
Stitching, stitching them together
A butterfly goes!

> *(Sora)*

Here, a striking metaphor is evident in comparing the fluttering of the butterfly with the act of stitching the rows of barley together. The uses of sign–mime can be exploited to help deaf students visualize the image, creating the necessary "picture in the mind." This can be done by joining the tips of the thumb and forefinger of one hand so as to shape an "O," keepingthe last three fingers outstretched and spaced apart. By fluttering the hand in the air, one can imitate the butterfly's flight – just as the great French mime, Marcel Maceau, popularized it on the stage. Also, it pantomimes the act of "sewing" – literally stitching the stalks of barley together while simultaneously imitating a butterfly fluttering in the air.

But there is more to the total imagery of the poem. What about the special sound effects in the repetition of "stitching"" Listen to what happens when you say the words! Do you feel anything, too? "I feel my teeth touching!" offers one student excitedly. "Yes!" bursts out another, "and I hear the sound of Clicking!" "Oh I know!" another student interjects. "The sound is like the clicking of a...of a...a stitching machine! When you say stitching, stitching them together, it's like your teeth were stitching the barley rows together, too!"

> *Up the barley rows, stitching, stitching*
> *them together a butterfly goes"*

It should be obvious that, in teaching poetry to the deaf, successful lesson implementation would include kinetic as well as oral interpretation. Hence the use of mime and the language of signs. When used coordinately and creatively, the technique becomes sign–mime, which literally "paints pictures in the air." The effect is to reproduce the very imagery of a poem so as to create a picture in the mind of the student. This is most important to concept development; it helps put together the pieces of the jig–saw puzzle, so to speak, and provides the gestalt or organizing principle which allows the student to grasp the full picture or whole meaning of the poem. The following may illustrate this:

> *One fallen flower*
> *Returning to the branch? Oh, no!*
> *A white butterfly!*
>
>   *(Moritake)*

The teacher has only to follow Hamlet's advice to the players, "Suit the action to the word," and the class will take it from there. Study the images of the poem....What do you see! "A tree and branches," says one student. Bending his left arm at the elbow, he makes the sign for "tree," fingers outstretched and pointing upward like branches. "A leaf is falling," and, fingers outspread like the points of a leaf, his right hand touches "the smallest branch" at the fingertips, "breaks off" and flutters downward. "But that is a leaf," chides another student, "it should be a flower!"

What about the butterfly? Do you see the comparison or metaphor? "Of course!" blurts out a third student, "The flower is the butterfly! We can use the same butterfly sign as in the other poem we did!" And she joins the tips of the thumb and forefinger of her right hand in the shape of an "O", this time, however, keeping the other three fingers close together (as in the letter "F" of the manual alphabet). "See the pretty white flower!" she says, admitting her handicraft. A slight twist, and it breaks off from the little finger branch of the left hand. "Now it falls to the earth," and her right hand floats downward, caressing the air until it comes to a stop. "Look! It's really a butterfly!" Suddenly, she opens the closed fingers of her right hand and starts it fluttering upwards. "Watch it return to the branch!" and the action completes the imagery and the meaning of the poem.

Having ventured this far into suggesting ways and means whereby poetry can serve as a useful tool in developing language power for deaf persons, it should be obvious that my methods of explication included the sign language and manual alphabet of the deaf. I do not see how it could be otherwise. It is the only possible medium through which profoundly deaf persons can be made to respond to the language of poetry.

Poetry, like music, was written to be heard. It was also written in the faith that there would always be people who were capable of reproducing its imagery, its rhythm, and its eloquence.

The ancient Greeks called them "rhapsodies" – gifted singers and interpreters of poetry – and the tradition has extended to the teacher in the classroom today. What good would all these poems be if the world had no such rhapsodies and teachers? Poetry would merely exist as printed words in a text and most likely would accumulate the dust of libraries and bookshelves as mute artifacts of a gloried past.

This would certainly be the experience of most deaf people, with the exception of those who became deafened in later years and who had once heard music. Yet, through the medium of their native language, the sign language, the deaf are capable of responding to beautiful word pictures, visual rhythms, and eloquent speech.

The composer needs the musician to interpret his sheet music into glorious song and symphony. Similarly, the poet would count it a rare honor to have the resourceful teacher make use of sign language and sign-mime to convey the riches of this poetic composition to those who cannot hear.

I think I have already demonstrated the value of oral methods in teaching poetry to the deaf and in developing their language skills. The potentialities of the sign language as a tool for optimum explication should also be utilized to its fullest. In doing so, the teacher would be using the true audio-visual approach, and this I firmly believe, is the most effective way of teaching poetry to the deaf.

As the poet, Ralph Waldo Emerson, best expressed this ideal in his poem, "Each and All"--

> "All is needed by each one,
> Nothing is pure or good alone:
>
> I caught the sparrow's note from heaven,
> Singing at dawn on the alder bough,
> I brought him home, in his nest, at even--
> He sings the song, but it cheers not now,
> For I didn't bring back the river and sky:
> He sang to my ear, they sang to my eye."

It is to be regretted that there is no way of illustrating in writing how sign language can reproduce the very imagery, the rhythm, and the eloquence of such poetry. This must be seen in actuality in order to be fully understood and appreciated. However, television offers real opportunity for teachers of the deaf to demonstrate the effectiveness of this technique, and video recordings can be witnessed near and far by any number of viewers who are thus enabled to relate to the verbal and the non-verbal contents of poetry. Only when this synthesis is achieved shall we all come to realize the significant of Keats' experience when he said, in his "Ode On A Grecian Urn"--

> "Thou still unravished bride of quietness,
> Thou foster child of Silence and slow Time,
> Sylvan historian, who canst thus express
> A flowery tale more sweetly than our rhyme...
>
> Heard melodies are sweet, but those unheard
> Are sweeter; therefore, ye soft pipes play on;
> Not to the sensual ear, but more endeared,
> Pipe to the spirit ditties of no tone."

Poetry thus provides a rich store of multisensory images for those of us laboring to relate the raw material of our life experiences to the shaping influences of the creative imagination. As the poet, Archibald Macleish, so aptly put it:

> *A poem should not mean*
> *But be.*

A poem communicates its meaning by the total impression it makes upon the five senses. The greater our involvement and responsiveness, the more meaningful the poem becomes and the deeper our appreciation. It is the teacher's responsibility to make this happen – to twang the five-stringed lyre within each student and turn them on with all kinds of vibrations. This is the essence of learning – if we are to get at the very root of the Latinate term educare, meaning "to draw out or from" the learner.

From such classroom dynamics, students can be motivated to do their own thing. Or, to paraphrase Marshall McLuhan, instead of having them merely read the poem, let them be the poem!

Furthermore, there is no better exercise for the imagination than in the reading of poetry. It will set our mind's eye "in a fine frenzy rolling," taking in new vistas of thought and of high endeavor. It will serve to stretch the imagination in such a way that our interests will be challenged and our curiosity piqued. We will be stimulated toward gaining newer and more gratifying experiences from life, and it will be our "open-sesame" to the world of culture. For what is culture if not an idealistic study of the life and times of famous characters, of famous places and things, and of the finer values in life?

Our knowledge will be enriched as we read the immortal tales of Homer or Virgil, of Dante and Milton. Some of the world's most celebrated love stories and tragedies, kingdoms and kings, will be revealed to our eyes, and we will sail on the high seas of adventure in quest of a buried treasure and once again unearth "the glory that was Greece, and the grandeur that was Rome." We will find that poetry is as much a part of history, and geography, and sociology and logic as is any other subject worth learning. Because poetry is the representation of life in all its various forms, in all its teeming personalities, and, accordingly, it will act as our guide to enlighten and to enhance anything that needs illustration in order to make real for us that fascinating story called, *Life*.

DEAF CHILDREN

Teaching the Deaf is less difficult than is
commonly supposed. We merely have to
introduce into their minds by way of the eye
what has been introduced into our own
by the ear.

Charles–Michael de l'Epée
1776

My Welcome to Your World of Silence
the birth of true communication between a mother and her deaf child
by
Elizabeth Ward

Hush is a soft caressing word,
Silence is a quiet word in itself,
Peace is a warm gentle word.

I think in words, draw comfort from them,
I rage with them, I weep with them,
I experience joy with them, disappointment with them,
Words are my shield, my lance, my defence and my attack,
I make friends with them, and enemies too,
I lend a helping hand with them or accept one,
I rebuke with them, or suffer rebuke in return,
Words were at my birth, they accompany my life,
Words are waiting for my death.

But you with your mind of pictures, colours movements.
Where are your words?
Your words are in your eyes, your smile, your tears, your frown.
Your hands reach out to try to touch my words,
I try to touch your colours; shapes I do not recognise bar my way,
Images move but do not speak.
I cannot see round your corners, in your hidden places.

But out of formless shadow comes the sign,
As out of darkness comes the dawn,
Light bears down on the moving forms, and illuminates the shades,
They stand out sure and firm against their background of colour.
They move – slowly – hesitantly,
The pattern they make is softly recognised,
My words dance with the shadows: they are understood.

A hush begins to grow, softly, safely.
There is a silence friendly in the air.
And Peace explodes.

words from a deaf child
by
Mervin Garretson

I need to perceive life through native eyes,
not yours, which after all, are yours.
you're sailing on a vastly foreign sea
it's my country – you're the stranger
listen to me.

we sign a language all our own
our hands are yours to share
the word, I think, is communication
and more than that, communion
we speak through sign and both together
whatever and by all the means to the end.

millions of stars do not make me a star
millions of dreams may not be my dream
the pilgrims were a handful on a newfound shore
that was their own.

let me choose if I will
to be different from the mass
learn that there is beauty in a single star
peace and grace in being what you are.

like an almighty wave this flash of scorn
for you who do not try to understand
that every sunset, every sunrise born
as different as each single grain of sand.

this life is yours to know but mine to command
teach me, love me, like you'd love a work of art
or a mountain pine
don't try to lead me, own me, force me
into a mold that's not my own.

water, feed, nourish the growing tree
don't hold it, fold it, circumscribe
let it flower, let it grow
if you love me, let me go.

Maternity Care for the Deaf
a Living Concern
by
Jennifer Kelsall

This paper describes an ongoing project to develop awareness of special needs of deaf mothers during, before and after childbirth.

The original teaching package which was researched with the help of my colleagues, Denise King and Debbie O'Grady at Wythenshaw Hospital, Manchester, was condensed into the book "Maternity Care for the Deaf" and printed by SWP in 1992. It is designed for the single purpose of enabling midwives, midwife teachers and midwifery students to improve the maternity care offered to mothers who are deaf or hearing impaired.

How Many Deaf Mothers are There?

A comment made several times by colleagues while we have been working on this project has been: "But we don't see many deaf mothers, do we?"

Is this a reason to further neglect this area of maternity care? Deaf and hearing-impaired mothers are a very small minority among the many thousands of hearing mothers that we seen every day. A deaf mother is already isolated by her disability and by becoming more aware of her problems and improving our communication skills we should be able to offer the deaf mother much better maternity care. The demand is no less urgent because it is not widespread. To meet what at times is an intense demand was the reason for developing our project.

In fact reliable incidence figures are hard to come by. They vary according to the definition of deafness. In the UK, the Institute of Hearing Research estimates 13.6 million people to have significant hearing loss and of these 423,000 are severely or profoundly deaf probably using some kind of gestural language.

The Hearing Research Trust estimate is some 7 million people with faulty hearing in the UK, 4 million subject to tinnitus and 1 in 1,00 born deaf. Of these it has been estimated that approximately 700 mothers with impaired hearing use the maternity services in the UK each year.

The fact that 50% of those older than 75 have some loss of hearing is irrelevant to our present concern with deaf motherhood.

Specialised Care

Good ante-natal care and education, expert care in labour and professional, competent care post-natally are the fundamental aims of sound midwifery practice. As midwives caring for maternity patients we can immediately see similarities amongst them but at the same time we are able to identify specific needs and worries – after all each mother is an individual and we try to adapt our care accordingly.

When a mother presents ante–natally with a disability her midwife immediately tries to tailor the maternity care to her requirements. The mother on crutches with her leg in plaster displays her disability and everyone is aware of the problems that could occur ante–natally, during labour or post–natally. Not so the deaf or hearing–impaired mother. The mother who is deaf has an unseen disability.

As midwives we are not always aware of the extent of the problem of deafness and care has too often been unwittingly inadequate.

To gain adequate information we approached deaf mothers and other professionals throughout the country. Their help and enthusiasm has enabled us to complete this project and we are indebted to them for their tremendous help.

The aim is to improve the awareness of the problems of deafness in relation to all aspects of midwifery and we offer suggestions and ideas whereby the care we give can be improved. The project work, from an initial idea to produce "a leaflet", snowballed to become a teaching pack and then this book and talks and articles have raised awareness of the needs of deaf parents throughout the UK.

Midwifery is essentially a practical art and to promote better care, allowing choice to deaf parents and their essential need for independence within a hearing society workshops and study days also provide further education in this field.

Midwives want to give the best care and through the project we have raised their deaf awareness to enable them to do this. Feedback from our initial teaching package suggests that this information has proved of great practical use and we are confident that the production of the book by Scottish Workshop Publications may extend the application of good practice in maternity care for deaf mothers.

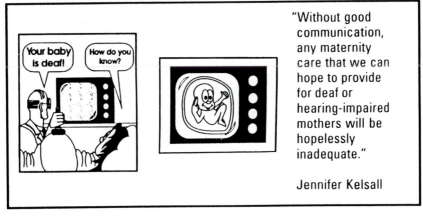

"Without good communication, any maternity care that we can hope to provide for deaf or hearing-impaired mothers will be hopelessly inadequate."

Jennifer Kelsall

Lottie Anderson

by
Agatha Tiegel – 1893

Once I sat me down and sighed,
Low and sad and weary,
And I said my life was dark,
And my work was dreary.
So I sat and murmured there
Longer and yet longer,
And forgot the courage high
That should make me stronger.
Then I raised my head and saw
Two eyes full of wonder,
Soft and bright and beautiful,
In expression tender.
And I felt my cheeks grow warm
With the shame of weakness,
And I rose rebuked and went
To my task with meekness.
Gracious little lady, thanks
For the lesson taught me.
Ever in her heart of hearts
Will thy teacher keep thee.

A Cup of Kindness
by
George Montgomery

Remembering Powrie Doctor

Powrie Vaux Doctor was born in 1903 in Scotch Plains, Kansas and died in action at the World Federation of the Deaf Congress in Paris, 1971.

Dr Doctor, for many years Dean of Graduate Studies, Professor and Chairman of the Department of Government at Gallaudet, was a pillar, more accurately several pillars, of higher education of deaf students in America and beyond. In 1994, whilst occupying the Chair in Deaf Studies that he founded, the present writer came across his monumental biography of Amos Kendall, the friend of Abraham Lincoln who gave his farmlands, Kendall Green, to the founding of a centre for the education of deaf students. This revealed some of the intellectual roots of "Doc's" total commitment to the advancement of Deaf people which I had admired and taken for a model during the last seven years of his life that I knew him. He talked of the origins of his concern with the deafness of his brother Frank Doctor but this was developed by study and direct experience of deaf communities all over the world into a rare philosophy of concern and commitment.

He was known to us outwith America as a one man world diplomatic service for deaf interests. Although he was not keen on travel for its own sake and never used air travel, he covered most of the world in his visits to work for deaf affairs. Some of the stories about his exploits have now acquired a legendary flavour, like his description of beef-tea and vodka issued as supplementary heating during a Winter journey on The Trans Siberian Railway. The present writer was attending a government reception in the northernmost corner of Europe in the Atrium of the Stadhuset, the parliament of Stockholm when across the well modulated controlled Swedish hubbub came a lusty Kansas bellow "M'NGAHMRY" and the throng parted like a Red Sea to reveal the jovial figure of Powrie homing in on the Scottish delegation. Others have recorded his ready repartee, as when one wit introduced him as Doctor Doctor to Dean Dean of the Catholic University of Washington; Powrie instantly regretted that they had not met in Pago-Pago. Whether ranging from Pago-Pago to Vladivostock, however, he never neglected to pay his, latterly, annual visits to the land of his forbears. His interest in Scotland was not superficial or sentimental. On learning that a teacher-training department was opened at Moray House College in Edinburgh, breaking the oralist monopoly of Manchester he rejoiced, proclaiming "God must be a Presbyterian after all." This was the nearest this pro-Catholic, Unitarian exemplar of toleration ever came to sectarian dogmatism but he followed it up with a more characteristic gesture of generosity when he bequeathed a considerable donation of books to lay down the seed corn of the specialist library in Deafness which still flourishes today in Moray House. Here, there was a personal and social dimension to common, intellectual, interests which is reflected in this reminiscence he shared with us at the end of his long and fruitful life:

For Auld Lang Syne

On returning home from a stay overseas one nearly always sums up in the mind's eye what one has seen and has learned and has experienced while traveling. Someway on the morning we sailed into New York harbor I kept hearing the song. "For Auld Lang Syne," as I watched the passengers saying good-bye on board ship. Perhaps the idea of returning home to old friends made me think of the song. Perhaps I was thinking of new friends I had made overseas. It might have been because I was thinking of old friends in Europe and I was unconsciously wondering when and if I should ever see them again.

The song took me back to the Military Tattoo at the Festival in Edinburgh, Scotland, which is always the highlight of the occasion. The Highland soldiers with their bagpipes, their swinging kilts, the Queen's own regiment in bear skin caps, the highland dances – all blending into a splendid pageant against the gray walls and turrets of Edinburgh Castle. At the conclusion of the spectacle the bands played the national anthems of various nations in the Commonwealth in which some of the audience joined in singing. When the bands played "God Save the Queen" hundreds of voices joined in the singing. However, as the last number the bands played "For Auld Lang Syne" and thousands of the spectators, Americans, English, Canadians, German, French, Irish – all joined hands with the Scots and sang. Truly this old song of the Scots is an international hymn.

The song reminded me of the time I was returning one evening from Tokyo to my ship in Yokahama Harbor in Japan. A Danish cruise ship was preparing to sail. The red Japanese sun and Mount Fujiyama loomed in the background. Colored streamers were flying from the ship as it slowly moved out into the harbor. The band played the Japanese and Danish national anthems, however, as the ship gathered speed the bands played "For Auld Lang Syne" and Japanese, Danes, Americans, Australians – all locked arms and sang together. Some way the words of the song united all the nationalities gathered on the docks in a way no flag could ever have done.

I remember years ago on Scotch Plains in Kansas how on New Year's Eve, we would take turns listening on the party telephone line. Bill Berry, who played the fiddle for the Scottish Country Dances, had a phonograph that played records of a cylinder shape that revolved like a wheel. He would give the party telephone line ring – one long ring, and everyone would take down the telephone receiver and listen to "Turkey and the Straw, Ha, Ha, Ha" and ".Annie Laurie." The program always concluded, however, with "For Auld Lang Syne."

I remember once asking my grandmother "Doc" if she had ever met old Mr. Lang Syne when she was living in Scotland. She explained to me that Lang Syne was no one's name but was the words of a song by Robert Burns and that the song asked us all to remember the good things that had happened during the past year and that especially we were to remember our friends. My grandmother said the song was really a blessing bestowed by all the Scots upon everyone in the world, and especially on New Year's Eve. And so on this New Year's Eve,

> *"We'll tak a cup o'kindness yet,*
> *For auld lang syne."*

Powrie Vaux Doctor
Gallaudet College
Kendall Green, 1970

Auld Lang Sign

Powrie Doctor's tireless efforts to promote the use of signs in the education of deaf children continued to bear fruit long after his death. Wondering about his possibly sub-conscious identification of "syne" and the homophonous "sign", led me to the following adaption of the Burns original. The sentiments expressed are nevertheless, no imitation, their direct sincerity deriving a lot from the observation of the inspired gusto my wife Joan Montgomery devoted to the deaf children she taught and cared for. We should like to dedicate it to the memory of Powrie Vaux Doctor, a true American, a true Scot, a true gentleman and a true friend.

Anthem for the World's Deaf Children
after Robert Burns

Should all deaf children be forgot,
And always last in line?
Should all deaf children be forgot,
And never taught to sign.

Nor seldom shown a sign of Love,
And often left to pine
Alone, without a helping hand
Until the end of time?

Give me your hand my trusty friend,
And here's a hand of mine.
We'll free the hand of each deaf child,
And teach them how to sign.

We'll free the mind of each deaf child,
Remember all the while
The light of learning in their eyes,
The sunshine in their smile.

"Vive la parole"
by Colin White

DEAF HISTORY
AND CULTURE

**"Those who do learn from the
past are condemned to relive it."**

G. Santayana

Of Roots and Wings...and the Family of Man
by
Jack Gannon

A tall, square, curved, rust-colored, metal sculpture stands in front of the Kendall Demonstration Elementary School for Deaf Children, on the Gallaudet University campus in Washington DC. This sculpture entitled, "Riding High", was the creation of Clement Meadmore, a hearing Australian-born sculptor. It was dedicated on June 16, 1982.

On that day a quotation by Hodding Carter (1907-1972), an American journalist and author, was used in the program. "There are only two lasting bequests we can hope to give our children", Carter had written. "One of these is roots; the other, wings." (The Kendall School has since adopted that quotation as a school theme.) Carter's statement is very symbolic of the importance of the Deaf history movement in the United States and abroad. As we Deaf people come to better understand our roots and ourselves, we are discovering our "wings".

Most of us have witnessed many changes within the Deaf community during our lifetime. Here in America we have seen our community grow from representation by a single national organization (the National Association of the Deaf), which for more than a century has represented the best interests of the majority of deaf people, into many organizations representing our community's diverse needs. Today, in addition to the NAD, we now have organizations representing the needs and interests of deaf women and native Americans, athletes, late deafened adults, Black Deaf and Deaf-Blind persons, gays and lesbians, hard of hearing individuals and other groups as our community comes to terms with and responds to its own diversity.

In the area of education, what was for a long time a heated controversy between an oral vs the sign language approach in teaching deaf children has grown into inclusion and mainstreaming and the role and future of our special or center schools. Since the National Association of the Deaf published Deaf Heritage in 1981, we have witnessed a ground swell of interest in Deaf history. Other history books have followed and we now have a Deaf Encyclopedia. We have seen this interest spill over among deaf persons searching for their Deaf family roots and their links to Deaf history.

Many of our center schools now offer classes in Deaf studies and this fall Gallaudet University will inaugurate a Department of Deaf Studies. The number of school museums focusing on d/Deaf history is also growing.

The growth of Deaf Awareness programs has created a demand for d/Deaf speakers and materials about deafness and deaf people. We have never before seen so many sign language books, dictionaries and videotapes, and mail order catalogues, plays and stage productions. The world is finally, slowly, learning about us.

During our generation we have witnessed a deaf actress win the coveted Oscar award and seen a deaf man elevated to the presidency of a university. We have seen the number of deaf persons with earned doctorates skyrocket and identified close to 20 deaf and hard of hearing school administrators and two directors of state departments. For the first time in our history a Deaf man has been tapped as assistant secretary of the Office of Special Education and Rehabilitive Services, the highest federal government position ever held by a deaf individual, and another now heads the National Captioning Institute. Deaf persons have addressed the United Nations and spoken before the Vatican, chaired national commissions and are serving on local and national school boards.

Technology, especially the computer, has brought deaf people almost instant access to information, and our bulletin board networks have quickened the exchange of information within the Deaf community and surpassed the speed of our famous "Deaf grapevine".

Most job announcements in the field of deafness or related fields now include the statement, "Qualified deaf and hard of hearing candidates are encouraged to apply." Our popular "I Love You" sign has gained wide appeal. It now appears on postage stamps, posters, apparel, jewelry and in popular figurines and dolls.

"Deaf Mosaic", Gallaudet's award-winning, monthly magazine-type television program which features d/Deaf people and their activities, is available in more than 65 million homes in the United States.

On the international level, The Deaf Way, a first-of-its-kind international festival and conference on the language, culture and history of Deaf people, held in the United States in 1989, attracted over 6,000 participants from 80 nations. An off-shoot of this event is a project spearheaded by Gallaudet University to erect and exhibit at an internationally known museum entitled, "DEAF: A Community of Signers." If this exhibit becomes a reality it will have the potential of being seen by millions of museum visitors.

One of the most significant historic events to occur during our lives took place at Gallaudet University in the spring of 1988. The importance of the "Deaf President Now" protest cannot be overestimated. It catapulted a Deaf man, Dr I King Jordan, into an international leadership role with his appointment as the first deaf president of Gallaudet University. It resulted in a change in the composition of the University's Board of Trustees with a 51% majority of deaf members and the selection of a deaf chairman. Some of the best deaf minds are now serving on that Board. What will be the outcome of this leadership? Time will tell.

The ripple effect of the "Deaf President Now" protest has gone well beyond the confines of Gallaudet's campus. President Jordan, for example, was the first person to testify before Congress in support of the Americans with Disabilities Act, and DPN has been credited with influencing the passage of this landmark legislation which will have an impact on the lives of people with disabilities everywhere.

DPN surprised and shook the world. Never before had such an event related to deaf people captured the world's attention. Suddenly hearing people began to look around then ask themselves, "where have all these deaf people been?" In many cases they were not aware that we even existed. How true. Those familiar with our history know what it has been like to be there, yet not involved or able to fully participate. Why does this keep happening? In large measure, I think because people do not have the opportunity to meet, interact with us on equal terms on an on-going basis.

Deaf history is gaining attention on the international level as well. In 1991 the first International Deaf History Conference was held at Gallaudet University. A year later the first European Symposium on Deaf History followed in Rodez, France. This October the 2nd International Conference on Deaf History will take place in Hamburg, Germany and is expected to result in the establishment of an international Deaf history organization. This conference will be followed in 1996 by the 2nd European Deaf History Symposium in Scotland. In Sweden and the United Kingdom deaf people have already established deaf history organizations.

Pride is a powerful thing. Most – if not all – successful people have an important sense of pride. They are proud of who they are or where they come from or proud of what they have accomplished or proud of some contribution they have made. This focus on our world has given us d/Deaf people an important identity. Our search for roots and the knowledge we are acquiring about ourselves and our history is changing us as individuals. This information gives us a greater "can-do-it" spirit and the desire to share this spirit with as many of our young people as we can and challenge them to greater heights.

Yet, in spite of all these advances and the good feelings many of us have about ourselves, we are still not full members of society or the "family of man". We are still deaf in a world dominated by sound. And, we are still struggling with one of the greatest hurdles of all – society's negative attitudes toward us deaf people.

Attitudes won't change until we start – and continue – talking about them. Misinformed, mistaken attitudes about deaf people will persist until people have the opportunity to get to know us, to work with us, to learn about and from us and to understand us and our rich legacy. And, unfortunately, these negative attitudes are so prevalent they are found even within our families, among loved ones and among people we generally consider well-informed. These attitudes are, of course, more commonplace in the field of employment and within the general population.

These attitudinal barriers remain as one of the most challenging hurdles of our time, and our success in overcoming them will largely determine whether or not we will become full, contributing members of society or remain, as we do today, on the fringes of mankind.

It is ironic, but just as we are discovering and documenting information about our roots on a wide scale, many deaf children are being placed in public schools or mainstream programs where they do not have access to that information! And, as "mainstreaming", or full inclusion, is occuring there is a move to dismantle or down-size our special/center schools which have played such a crucial role in making us the individuals we are.

Another irony of mainstreaming deaf children in the public school is the mistaken belief that it helps "normalize" deaf children and better prepares them to become members of society. As so many of us know from our personal experiences, what too often happens is that placing deaf children in the public school only isolates them further and denies them access to effective communication and a solid education. While the use of interpreters is very helpful, interpreters can never replace a trained teacher who can teach and communicate directly with her/his students. This move to the mainstream also denies deaf children the benefit of skilled, knowledgeable deaf teachers who understand them, are one of them and serve as important role models.

So, it boils down to this: how can we D/deaf people truly be members of the family of man and accept and respect each others' values when our own native language and our values are not considered important, nor respected or accepted? This summer I was pleasantly surprised and touched on a visit back home to learn that my nephew and nieces had taken it upon themselves to learn fingerspelling so they could better communicate with my wife and me. While communicating with the elderly members in the family was still by the slow hit-and-miss lipreading process, communicating with the younger generation was a pure delight. When my older brother displayed impatience with my inability to lipread what he was saying, I found it strange that I had to remind him that he could learn to fingerspell while I couldn't learn to hear.

If the younger generation can assume this type of common sense leadership, is it not the time to again think seriously about the possibility of teaching sign language in our schools? This is not a new or novel idea. Deaf leaders have been proposing including sign language in our schools for generations. In this age of accessibility and sensitivity to people with disabilities perhaps the time for it to happen is now. I think the World Federation of the Deaf and our national associations should take the lead and make this a priority.

Here in the United States, American Sign Language has taken on a new dimension. The "Deaf President Now" movement exposed millions of television viewers to our visual language, and after the protest there was a noticeable surge in the number of persons interested in learning sign language. As estimated 1,000 colleagues and universities in the United States now offer some kind of course in sign language or manual communication.

We are seeing an increased number of educational workshops and conferences and many educators are searching for the best way to teach ASL and English. At several national disability conferences I have attended I have encountered more and more hearing individuals who can fingerspell. Fingerspelling, as we know, is often the first step in learning our language. This change tells me that people with disabilities and professionals who work with them are indeed, gradually becoming sensitive to the communication needs of deaf people.

Gallaudet's National Information Center on Deafness reports that at least 17 states currently have laws recognizing American Sign Language as a "foreign language". In 1983 Sweden became the first nation to recognize its sign language – Swedish Sign Language – as a national language. The European Parliament also recognises sign language and in 1993 Ontario, Canada became the first country in North America to recognise American and French sign languages as languages of instruction for deaf and hard of hearing students. I am optimistic enough to believe that other states and nations will follow these leads.

Thanks to those who have studied our language thoroughly, we now know that American Sign Language is a language. It is no longer what critics used to call "a collection of wild gestures". It is a beautiful, expressive, visual language. It is the root of a rich culture and history. It is finally gaining the acceptance and the respect that it deserves. Why, then, cannot our sign language be taught in all public schools? The number of deaf people in any single nation is large enough to warrant it.

If the powers-that-be insist on mainstreaming deaf children in public school, then do we not have a right to insist that these schools use communication accessible to these children and teach sign language so that the deaf students' hearing classmates, teachers and school personnel can communicate with them?

Teaching sign language in our public schools would not only make education more accessible to deaf children, but it would produce generations of future co-workers, neighbors, merchants, professionals, doctors, lawyers and others with, at the very least, functional knowledge of our language and skill to communicate with us. In the process of learning our language others will learn about us and see us as the diverse individuals we are.

Until there is effective communication between deaf and hearing students and teachers, deaf students will continue to be shortchanged and isolated. Only with effective two-way communication will we deaf and hard of hearing people truly be able to assume our role as contributing members to society.

Let me conclude with a story I have used in many of my presentations. There was a young deaf girl about 11 or 12 years old at the school where my wife and I used to teach (which, incidentally, is one of the schools presently threatened with closure). One day she was introduced to a high-ranking state education official in the hallway of the school building. After the introduction, this official looked at her and asked, "Do you wish you could hear?"

The unusual question caught the young lass, who had been born deaf, by surprise. She thought seriously for a moment then she shook her head and responded forthrightly, "No, but I wish I could fly!". I love that young girl's response. It sums up one's perspective of life so well and is so typical of the thinking of the many deaf people I have had the pleasure of knowing.

Yes, we must give our deaf children their roots so they can develop their "wings". We want them not only to be able to "fly", but to soar to greater heights ... and take their rightful place in the family of man.

Dr Gannon is the author of two popular books, Deaf Heritage, A Narrative History of Deaf America and The Week the World Heard Gallaudet. Deafened at the age of eight, he is a graduate of the Missouri School for the Deaf and Gallaudet University. He holds an honorary doctorate from Gallaudet University where he is Special Assistant to the President for Advocacy.

Isolation Experiments on Children's Language
by
Robert Grieve

Introduction

Students of children's language development are familiar with three isolation experiments – where children are isolated at birth and prevented from overhearing spoken language for a number of years – allegedly conducted in ancient mediaeval times. Both Marx (1967) and Blumenthal (1976) refer to such experiments, allegedly conducted by a pharaoh, Psamtik I, in the seventh century BC; by a King of Sicily, Frederick II, in the thirteenth century AD; and by a king of Scotland, James IV, in the fifteenth century AD.

Did these experiments ever take place, or are these accounts merely fabulous? In this chapter the accounts of the experiments will be examined to see if they are authentic. A fourth experiment, by a moghul emperor in India, Akbar the Great, in the sixteenth century AD, will also be considered, particularly as it seems little known to students of children's language. The research described here derives from work completed in collaboration with my colleague Dr Robin Campbell of the University of Stirling (Campbell and Grieve, 1982).

In examining the authenticity of the following accounts, a main factor to be borne in mind is that the accounts of the experiments at least need to be contemporary with the experiments they describe, and the accounts need to have been written by those with some intimate knowledge of the royal courts at which the experiments supposedly took place.

The Egyptian Study

The first account of an isolation experiment comes from Herodotus (Powell, 1949), and it is as follows:

Investigator: Psamtik 1, Egypt, 7th Century BC

Now until Psammetichus reigned over them, the Egyptians believed that they were the eldest of all men. But ever since Psammetichus became king and resolved to learn who were indeed the eldest, they have believed that the Phrygians were before them, but they themselves before the rest. For when Psammatechus was not able by enquiring to learn the answer from any man, he conceived this device. He gave two new–born babes or ordinary men to a shepherd, to nurture among his flocks after this manner. He charged him that none should utter any speech before them, but they should live by themselves in a solitary habitation; and at the due hours the shepherd should bring goats to them, and give them their fill of milk, and perform the other things needful. Thus Psammetichus did and commanded because he desired, when the babes should be past meaningless whimperings, to hear what tongue they would utter first. And these things came to pass; for after the shepherd had wrought thus for a space of two years, when he opened the door and entered in, both babes fell down before him, and cried *becos*, and stretched out their hands. Now when the shepherd heard it the first time, he held his peace; but when this word was oftentimes spoken as he came to care for them, then he told his lord, and brought the children into his presence when he commanded. And when Psammatechus had also heard it, he enquired which nation called anything *becos*; and enquiring, he found that the Phrygians call bread by this name. Thus the Egyptians, guided by this sign, confessed that the Phrygians were elder than they. That so it came to pass I heard of the priests of Hephaestus in Memphis.

Chronicler: Herodotus, 5th Century BC

The problem with this account is immediately apparent. The experiment was allegedly conducted by Psamtik – often referred to as 'Psammatechus' – in the seventh century BC, but the chronicler, Herodotus, is writing in the fifth century BC. The account is therefore far from contemporary. Moreover, Herodotus is quite explicit that his account is based on hearsay, for he tells us that he was told this tale by priests at Memphis.

How likely is it that Psamtik would have conducted such an experiment? This is difficult to answer, for little seems to be known about him, though he did seem to have an inquiring turn of mind, evidenced by his attempt to identify the source of the Nile.

How likely is it that the tale of the experiment is a fabrication? There are two forms of support for this. One is that the tale of such an experiment was evident in ancient times, details of people and places varying. The second is that in ancient Egypt, it was apparently acceptable to poke fun at the gods and at the pharaohs. The tale may therefore be no more than a jocular invention, intended to poke fun at the pharaoh, on the ground that his experiment backfired. He conducted the experiment to show that the Egyptians were the oldest race. To do so he isolated children from language, in the belief that they would come to speak the original language of the oldest race – ie Egyptian. But look what happened – they came to speak Phrygian, and the pharaoh had to concede that the Egyptians were not the oldest race.

The Sicilian Study

The account of the second experiment is by Salimbene (Coulton 1907), and it is as follows:

Investigator: Frederick II, Sicily, 13th Century AD

Like Psammetichus, in Herodotus, he make linguistic experiments on the vile bodies of hapless infants, bidding foster-mothers and nurses to suckle and bathe and wash the children, but in no wise to prattle or speak with them; for he would have learnt whether they would speak the Hebrew language (which had been the first), or Greek, or Latin, or Arabic, or perchance the tongue of their parents of whom they had been born. But he laboured in vain, for the children could not live without clappings of the hands, and gestures, and gladness of countenance, and blandishments.

Chronicler: Salimbene, 13th Century AD

This account looks more hopeful as regards authenticity, in the sense that Salimbene, a friar in the church, was a contemporary of Frederick. However, he was not an intimate of the court, and his personal knowledge of Frederick was limited to a glimpse he caught of the king as he proceeded through Parma in 1235.

How likely is it that Frederick would have conducted the experiment attributed to him? The initial answer here is positive, for Frederick is known to have been greatly interested in language – reputedly speaking nine languages and being literate in seven. He is also known to have been interested in the merits of direct observation, and Arabic scholars of science, mathematics and astronomy were welcomed to his court.

On the other hand, the case for the alleged experiment being a fabrication is also strong. Not to put too find a point on it, Frederick's court and the church did not get on. He was excommunicated by Pope Gregor IX for failing to pursue the Crusaders with sufficient vigour. Far from deprecating or wishing to slay the infidel, Frederick welcomes Arabic scholars and scientists to his court, as just mentioned. There was therefore tension and conflict between court and church. When we recall that Salimbene was a friar in the church; that his account of the children's isolation experiment is set amongst a list of other cruel deeds attributed to Frederick (eg, the cutting off of a notary's thumb for mis-spelling his name, the shutting up of a man in a wine barrel to see what would happen to his soul on death); and the reported outcome of the alleged experiment: the children died – this may be no more than a malicious invention in a propaganda war between church and court.

The Scottish Study

The chronicler here is Sir Robert Lindesay of Pitscottie, usually referred to simply as 'Pitscottie'. His account (Mackay, 1899/1931) is as follows:

Investigator: James IV, Scotland, 15th Century AD

The king gart tak ane dum woman and pat hir in Inchekeytht and gaif hir tua zoung bairnes in companie witht hir and gart furnische them of all necessar thingis pertening to thair nurischment that is to say, meit, drink, fyre and candell, claithis, witht all wther kynd of quhat langage thir bairnes walk speik quhene they come to lauchfull aige. Sum sayis they spak goode hebrew bot as to myself I knaw not bot be the authoris reherse. (Thir actis foirsaid was done in the zeir of god imiiij'lxxxxiij zeiris.) (1493)

Chronicler: Pitscottie, 16th Century AD

(The king (James IV) put a dumb womb woman in Inchkeith, and gave to her two young children, and furnished them with life's necessities for nourishment – meat, drink, fire, candles and clothes and with all other required necessities to man or woman – wishing by this means to know what language the children would speak when they came to lawful age. Some say they spoke good Hebrew, but as to myself I know nothing except what I have been told. (These foresaid acts were done in the year of god 1493.)

With regard to authenticity, though we now have a place – Inchkeith, an island in the Firth of Forth, and a date – 1493, the problem is again immediately apparent. Pitscottie's chronicle was written in the sixteenth century, about events alleged to have taken place in the fifteenth century. His account is therefore not contemporary. In addition, like Herodotus, he is quite explicit that the tale is based on hearsay: 'I knaw not bot be the authors reherse' – 'I know nothing except what I have been told'.

The likelihood of James being the sort of individual to have conducted such an experiment is in some respects high. Like Frederick, he was very interested in language, reputedly speaking seven languages apart from English. He was certainly interested in science, establishing what Read (1938a, 1938b, 1947) describes as the first laboratory in Scotland, established by James IV at Stirling Castle, to study the turning of base metals into gold – alchemy!

But again, the likelihood of the tale being fabulous is also high. The reported outcome – that the children came to speak Hebrew – is perhaps no more than a jocular invention, designed to poke fun at those who thought Hebrew to be the original language: an idea not uncommon in mediaeval times.

The Indian Study

Here we are on quite different ground as regards authenticity. In cases of experiments attributed to Psamtik, Frederick, and James, it has been noted that there is a lack of authentication through the lack of accounts of contemporary chroniclers who were intimates of the courts of these monarchs. This is not the case with accounts of Akbar's experiment. Here we have three accounts, each contemporary, and each provided by individuals intimately involved with Akbar's court.

Before presenting these accounts, a word about Akbar. He did not accept orthodox Islam, and spent a considerable period of his life seeking an appropriate, alternative religious faith. Apparently he was unable to read, but enjoyed a library of over twenty thousand books and manuscripts which were read to him. He thought that issues would be settled not by experiment, but by debate, and he had an elaborate debating hall built for this purpose.

Nonetheless, an isolation experiment on children's language is attributed to him. The three accounts are provided by Xavier, the leader of the Jesuit mission invited to Akbar's court to explain christianity (recall Akbar's seeking of an appropriate faith to follow); by Badauni, a member of Akbar's court who published a history of his reign after Akbar's death (Badauni disapproved of Akbar's failure to subscribe to orthodox Islam); and by Abu'l-Fazl, who was secretary and prime minister at Akbar's court, and who published a history of Akbar's reign, the Akbarnama. The accounts are those of McLagan, 1932; Lowe, 1884; Beveridge, 1888:

Investigator: Akbar, India, 16th Century AD

Chronicler: Xavier, 16th Century AD

He told me that nearly 20 years ago he had 30 children shut up before they could speak, and put guards over them so that the nurses might not teach them their language. His object was to see what language they would talk when they grew older. He was resolved to follow the laws and customs of the country who language was that spoken by the children. But his endeavours were a failure, for none of the children came to speak distinctly. Wherefore at this time he allowed no law but his own.

Chronicler: Badauni, 16th Century AD

At this time they brought a man to Court, who had no ears nor any trace of the orifices of the ear. In spite of this he heard everything that was said to him, though the place of the ears was quite level. And in this year, in order to verify the circumstances of this case, an order was issued that several suckling infants should be kept in a secluded place far from habitations, where they should not hear a word spoken. Well-disciplined nurses were to be placed over them, who were to refrain from giving them any instructions in speaking, so as to test the accuracy of the tradition which says:

"Every one that is born is born with a natural tendency", by ascertaining what religion and sect these infants would incline to and above all what creed they would repeat. To carry out this order about twenty sucklings were taken from their mothers, for a consideration in money, and were placed in an empty house, which got the name of "Dumb-house". After

three or four years they all turned out dumb and the appellation of the place turned out prophetic. Many of these sucklings became the nurselings of mother earth:

My mother is earth, and I am a suckling,
The propensity of children for their mother is strange,
Soon will it be that resting from trouble
I shall fall drunk with sleep on my mother's bosom.

Chronicler: Abu'l-Fazl, 16th Century AD

One of the occurrences was the testing of the silent of speech. There was a great meeting, and every kind of enlightenment was discussed. In the 24th Divine year (1578) HM said that speech came to every tribe from hearing, and that each remembered from another from the beginning of existence. If they arranged that human speech did not reach them, they certainly would not have the power of speech. If the fountain of speech bubbled over in one of them, he would regard this as Divine speech, and accept it as such. As some who hear this appeared to deny it, he, in order to convince them, had a serai built in a place which civilized sounds did not reach. The newly born were put into that place of experience, and honest and active guards were put over them. For a time tongue-tied wet nurses were admitted there. As they had closed the door of speech, the place was commonly called the Gang Mahal (the dumb-house). On the 9th August 1582 he went out to hunt. That night he stayed in Faizabad, and next day he went with a few special attendants to the house of experiment. No cry came from that house of silence, nor was any speech heard there. In spite of their four years they had no part of the talisman of speech, and nothing came except the noise of the dumb. What the wise Sovereign had understood several years before was on this day impressed on the hearts of the formalists and the superficial. This became a source of instruction to crowds of men. HM said,

"Though my words were proved, they still are saying the same things with a tongueless tongue. The world is a miserable abode of species. To shut the lips is really to indulge in garrulity. They have hamstrung the camel of the Why and Wherefore, and have closed the gate of speech with iron walls."

Verse

Enough, Nizami, be silent of discourse, Why speak
to a world with cotton in its ears,
Shut your demonstrations into a narrow phial,
Put them all in a phial and place a stone thereon.

So, an isolation experiment on children's language has been conducted – by Akbar the Great, Moghul Emperor, in India, at Faizabad, from 1578–82.

Ironically, Akbar is the least likely experimental investigator. Psamtik possibly, Frederick and James certainly, are likely candidates for the conduct of such an experiment, given their known inquiring turn of mind, and in the cases of Frederick and James, their interests in language and observation and experiment. Akbar thought that issues were to be decided by debate, not one generation to the next. Prevent that (eg, in an isolation experiment), and no language would ensue. He arranged this, and found that no language ensued. But was he believed? No, 'the world is a miserable abode of sceptics'. i.e., conduct an experiment, and folk nevertheless fail to believe you. So place a stone on the efficacy of experiments.

But he did conduct the experiment, for we have three contemporary accounts by intimates of his court.

The outcome? Abu'l-Fazl tells us that : 'nothing came out except the noise of the dumb', and Xavier tells us that : 'none of the children came to speak distinctly'.

What do these intriguing phrases mean: 'the noise of the dumb', 'to speak distinctly' If there was silence, then why not say so, as Badauni implies? But Abu'l-Fazl and Xavier do not say this. Instead, we have their intriguing phrases. Here it can be observed that if the isolated children had invented a language, then by definition no one would recognise it. Is it an invented language that Xavier is alluding to – lack of distinct speech?; and that Abu'l-Fazl describes – 'the noise of the dumb'?

Conclusion

Three isolation experiments on children's language – where children are isolated, from birth, for several years from over-hearing language – are reasonably well known: the studies in ancient and mediaeval times of Psamtik I, the pharaoh of Egypt in the seventh century BC; of Frederick II, king of Sicily in the thirteenth century AD; and of James IV, king of Scotland in the fifteenth century AD. Here it has been argued that the tales of these experiments could be fabulous – jocular or malicious inventions.

In the case of a little known fourth experiment, that of Akbar in India in the sixteenth century, there is reliable evidence that the experiment was conducted, from three different chroniclers who were intimates of the court. The historical point is thus established: an isolation experiment on children's language has been conducted, by Akbar. The outcome, though, remains unclear. What do the chroniclers mean when they tell us that 'none of the children came to speak distinctly', and that 'nothing came out (of the place of the experiment) except the noise of the dumb'? Nothing of interest? or a novel, invented language, unrecognised? While the research reported here answers the historical question, it does not, however, answer the scientific question on the effect of the environment on children's language development.

References

Beveridge H (1888) Father Jerome Xavier. Journal of the Asiatic Society of Bengal, 57, 1-38.

Blumethal A L (1976) Language and psychology: historical aspects of psycholinguistics. New York: Wiley.

Campbell R N and Grieve R (1982) Royal investigations of the origin of language. Historiographia Linguistica, IX, 43-74.

Coulton G G (1907) From St Francis to Dante. London: Nutt.

Lowe W H (1884) Translation of Volume II of Badauni's Muntakhab-ut-Tawarikh. Bibliotheca Indica Series. Asiatic Society of Bengal.

Mackay A J G (1899/1931) Pitscottie's Historie and Chronicles of Scotland. Edinburgh: Blackwood.

MacLagan E D (1932) The Jesuits and the Great Moghul. London: Burns, Oates and Washbourne.

Marx O (1967) The history of biological bases of language. In E H Lenneberg, Biological Foundations of Language. New York: Wiley.

Powell J E (1949) Herodotus' Histories. Oxford: Clarendon.

Read J (1938a) Alchemy in Scotland. The Chemist and Druggist. (25 June), 1–4.

Read J (1938b) Alchemy under James IV of Scotland. Ambix 2, 60–67.

Read J (1947) Humour and humanism in chemistry. London: Bell.

Errare Humanum Est

Some Corrections of American and British
Publications on the History of the
Education of Hearing-Impaired Children
by
Armin Löwe

Although the number interested in the history of the education of hearing-impaired children has greatly increased recently, the number of professional people who have this special interest and, therefore, are attentive readers of corresponding publications remains comparatively small. This is true of European professionals and perhaps even more of professional people in North America. As a–now retired–professor of paedo-audiology and education of deaf children at the Department of Special Education within the University of Education at Heidelberg, I had to occupy myself again and again with the historical aspects of these two disciplines and to study old and new literature on them not only in my German mother-tongue but also in foreign languages. And because I have a special interest in the comparative education of hearing-impaired children I consulted also a number of books written by American and/or British authors.

To my great surprise, I identified in these books an unexpectedly large number of false statements and inferences. In this short contribution I want to direct the attention of American and British readers to some of them. My only intention in pointing them out is the desire to interrupt, if possible, their passing-on from one generation to the next.

My comments are based on the following publications listed in alphabetical order.

RUTH BENDER

The Conquest of Deafness. A History of the Long Struggle to Make Possible Normal Living to Those Handicapped by Lack of Normal Hearing. Third Edition. Danville/Illinois 1981.

1.   "Born in 1520, of a noble family, Ponce de León, interested himself, as a young man, in the education of deaf-mutes." (p. 36).

Pedro Ponce de León was not born in 1520. The correct year is 1529.

2.   "It was in the court of King Philip that Luis de Valesco encountered Prince Charles of England. James 1 hoped to unite England and Spain in a pact of peace, after the disastrous Thirty Years War, by the marriage of his son to the Infanta of Spain. In 1623, Charles, the Prince of Wales, and the Duke of Buckingham made the trip to pay court to the Spanish princess ...". (p. 41).

The "Thirty Years War" lasted from 1618 till 1648 and was not finished in 1623.

3.   August Friedriche Petschke (1759-1822) "later became the director of the school at Leipzig (...). He advocated forming a community of deaf-mutes, even after their education was completed, where they might live together and earn their living by some sort of manufacturing project, in a sheltered workshop." (p. 104).

Ruth Bender specifies as source for this statement the book "De l'education des sourds-muets de naissance" (Volume 1, p. 34-35) which was written by Joseph Marie Degerando (1772-1842) and published in 1827. Either Ruth Bender or Joseph Marie Degerando is incorrect. August Friedrich Petschke did not propose to bring together deaf-mute persons in so called labour colonies and to offer them special places of work. This proposal was made by Dr Ludwig Grasshoff (1770-1851) in his publication "Beitrag zur Lebenserleichterung der Taubstummen durch Gründung einer taubstummengemeinde" (1820) (=Contribution to the facilitation of life through the formation of a community of deaf-mutes).

4.   "In May of 1828, while studying in Berlin, he (=Friedrich Moritz Hill) heard an announcement concerning a course for teaching deaf-mutes. This caught his interest in such earnest that in 1830 he entered the old Heinicke institute at Weissenfels, where he remained until death in 1874." (p. 126).

The small school for deaf children at Weissenfels which was attached to the teachers' training college was opened in 1829, ie 39 years after the death of Samuel Heinicke (1727-1790), who was the first principal of the school for deaf children at Leipzig from 1778 till 1790. Friedrich Moritz Hill (1805-1874) did not want to become a teacher for deaf children. How much he had disliked this idea, can be seen from his own words.

"A lurid shadow case on my life and striving, when I was given order by the ministry to attend the school for the deaf in Berlin as a so called trainee from the 1st of October of 1829 and to prepare myself for the profession of a teacher of the deaf. I obeyed this order, although with an inner resistance, but did not find any satisfaction. (...) It hit me like a crash of thunder, when I was told in July of 1830 (...) that I was designated for the vacant position of the first teacher at the school for the deaf at Weissenfels and that I have to assume my duties on the 1st of October on this year." (Translation of a quotation. In: Walther 1882, P. 286-387).

5.   "In the northern countries, the most rapid progress was made in Denmark, with the state foundation for schools for the deaf by 1807. Education for deaf children was compulsory by 1840." (p. 134).

Compulsory education for hearing-impaired children was realized in Denmark in 1817. In his contribution on the education of deaf children in Denmark to the book "Das Taubstummenbildungwesen im XIX. Jahrhundert in den wichtigsten Staaten Europas" (=The education of deaf children during the 19th century in the most important countries of Europe), edited by Johannes Karth (1863-1950) in 1902, Georg Forchhammer (1861-1938) offers the following information:

"(...) the school was founded (...) as Royal Institute on the 17th of April of 1807 (...). The Institute grew rapidly, in particular after 1817, when compulsory education was introduced also for deaf-mute children in the whole country. Since that time (1817) all deaf-mutes of the country have received instruction." (p. 204).

6.   "The nuns from Cabra, Ireland, carried the work to New South Wales in 1875 (...)." (p. 135).

With this sentence Ruth Bender wants to say that the education of deaf children in Australia was started by nuns from Ireland. This is, however, not true. The first two schools for deaf children in Australia were already founded in 1860, one in Melbourne and one in Sydney, as can be read in the historical monograph "Story of the Victorian School for the Deaf Children," written by J H Burchett and published in 1964:

"This history is more than the story of the Victorian School for Deaf Children (formerly the Victorian Deaf and Dumb Institution) – it tells the very genesis of deaf education in Australia as the New South Wales Institution for the Deaf was founded in the same year." (p. 1).

The Victorian School for Deaf Children in Melbourne was opened on the 12th of November of 1860.

7. "The Abba Serafino Balestra (1834–1886) was in charge of the school at Como (...). In 1867, he went to Rotterdam to see the work of David Hirsch. What he saw convinced him of the value of oralism. He went back to Italy, where he did all he could to spread oral teaching of the deaf of his own country.
"Eventually, he went to South America, to Buenos Aires. There, he opened the first school for the deaf at that continent." (P. 151).

When I was lecturing in the Argentine in 1977, I could collect the following information on the beginning of the education of deaf children in Latin America: "Domingo F Sarmiento (1811–1888), who became president of the Republic of the Argentine in 1868 and who was a trained teacher, had opened the first South American school for the deaf children in Chile, where he lived in exile at that time, in 1843. After he could return to the Argentine later on where he was elected first senator and then president, he was always a sponsor of the education of the deaf. Therefore, the education of the deaf can look back in the Argentine on a history or more than 100 years. It is of special interest for German teachers of the deaf, that the first school for deaf children in the Argentine was founded in Buenos Aires in 1857 by Karl Keil, a German teacher of the deaf. He had imported the German method of oral education to the Argentine." (Löwe 1977, p. 144–145).

8. "With the Nazi regime in 1933, the education of the handicapped took a different place in the scheme of things. Books on special education were ordered burned, and many of them were." (p. 162).

When I doubt the correctness of this statement, I do not intend to play down the cruelties of the National Socialist regime and to make them to look harmless. On the contrary, I could never do this alone for that reason that two of my relatives were victims of the euthanasia, as the National Socialists called their "mercy killing" program. But nowhere did I hear or read that books on the education of deaf children in particular and on the education of handicapped children in general were burnt during the so called "action against the un-German spirit" which was ordered by Joseph Goebbels, the National Socialist minister for the education of people and for propaganda and which took place on the 10th of May of 1933. Even after 1933 a number of books on special education were published in Germany, among them the voluminous "Geschichte des Taubstummenwesents" (1940), written by Paul Schumann (1870–1943). And since 1934 a new professional journal – it was brought into line with the philosophy of the National Socialism – was edited for all teachers of handicapped children. Its title was "Die Deutsche Sonderscule" (=the German special school).

9. "Paul Schumann who in 1927 had participated in a celebration honouring Heinicke at Leipzig (...)." (p. 163).

The bicentennial convention of the Association of German Teachers of the Deaf on the occasion of the 200th birthday of Samuel Heinicke in 1927 did not take place at Leipzig but at Hamburg.

10.   Ruth Bender concludes her book with a chronological chart. Unfortunately, it contains several false and many incomplete year dates. Here I want to rectify only the most important of them:

Pedro Ponce de León: he did not live from 1520 till 1584, but from 1510 till 1584 (Perello).

Juan Pablo Bonet: he did not live from 1579 till 1620, but from 1579 till 1633 (Perello, Schumann).

Manuel Ramirez de Carrión: he did not live from 1615 till 1619, but from 1579 till 1652 (Perello, Schumann).

Anton Deusing: he lived from 1612 till 1666 (Shumann).

Franz Mercurius van Helmont: he lived from 1614 till 1699 (Schumann).

R. Ernaud: he lived from 1740 till 1800 (Perello).

Johann Ludwig Ferdinand Arnoldi: he lived from 1737 till 1783 (Schumann).

Etienne Francois Deschamps: he lived from 1745 till 1791 (Perello, Shumann).

Viktor August Jäger: he lived from 1794 till 1864 (Schumann).

Karl Ferdinand Neumann: he did not live from 1812 till 1827, but from 1788 till 1833 (Schumann).

Zenas Freeman Westervelt: he lived from 1849 till 1918 (Western New York Institution for Deaf-Mutes).

DARCY M C DALE

Individualised Integration. Studies of Deaf and Partially-hearing Children and Students in Ordinary Schools and Colleges. London 1984.

1.   "An inspector of schools in Saxony, J B Graser published 'The Deaf Mute Restored to Society through Lipreading and Speech' in 1829 (...)." (p. 28).

Johann Baptist Graser (1766–1841) was inspector of schools first at Bamberg and then Bayreuth. Both cities are situated in Bavaria and not in Saxony.

NORMAN ERBER

Auditory Training. Washington DC. 1982.

1.   "In the 1950s and 60s, the 'Auditory Global Method' was developed, applied and promoted by Wedenberg (1951, 1954), Hulzing (1959), Ewing & Ewing (1961), Whetnall & Fry (1964), van Uden (1970) and Simmons (1971) (see Calvert & Silverman, 1975). This approach to the use of a child's hearing capacity combines aided listening and lipreading. (...). The Auditory Global Method represented a departure from the earlier acoustic methods in two respects. First, the pupils were encouraged to look as well as to listen most of the time. Second, (...)." (p. 4–5).

Not all professional people who are enumerated by Erber as representatives of the "Auditory Global Method" encouraged their pupils to look and to listen at the same time; on the contrary, some of them tried to avoid this directly. This is especially true of Erik Wedenberg (born 1905) and also of Edith Whetnall (1910–1966). Wedenberg points plainly in one of his publications to the fact that his method of auditory learning "is built primarily and principally upon the auditory sense with the visual sense as a complement, in contrast to other methods based upon the visual sense first with the auditory sense as a complement" (Wedenber 1954, p. 31).

Wedenberg gets also the facts very clear that there is a difference between his predominantly unisensory beginning and the bisensory approach recommended by Ewing & Ewing: "Educating a child auditorially regardless of the degree of auditory impairment deviates from the principles interpreted by Ewing among others." (1954, p. 17).

MARILYN FRENCH-ST. GEORGE and RICHARD STOKER

Speechreading: An Historical Perspective. In: The Volta Review, 90 (5/1988), P. 17–31.

1.   "The first British school for the deaf was opened by Thomas Braidwood in 1767." (p. 19).

All European publications on the history of the education of the deaf agree upon the year in which the first British school for deaf children was opened, namely in 1760. I want to quote only two of them:

"(...) and at the same time at which the institute of Paris was founded, opened Thomas Braidwood in 1760 the first school for the deaf at Edinburgh." (Emmerig 1927, p.138).

"The first school for the Deaf and Dumb in Britain was set up at Edinburgh in 1760 by Thomas Braidwood." (Ballantyne & Martin 1984, p. 187).

2.   "(...) the 1881 international conference of educators of the deaf in Milan declared that all educational programs for the deaf should encourage the development of oral communication." (p. 19).

The second international congress of teachers of the deaf in Milan did not take place in 1881 but one year earlier, namely from the 6th till the 11th of September of 1880. This follows unmistakably not only from the published report of Edmund Treibel (1881) but also from

Richard Brill's book on "International Congresses on Education of the Deaf – An Analytical History 1878–1980" (1984).

3.   "(...) Graser (1766–1841), who opened the integration class for normal–hearing and hearing–impaired children in 1821, (...)." (p. 24).

Johann Baptist Graser had set up the first self–contained class of hearing–impaired children within the building of an elementary school for hearing children at Bayreuth in 1821. This class was placed into a regular school, but it was not a mixed class of hearing and of hearing–impaired children.

4.   "Johann Konrad Ammann (1669–1730) encouraged his students to look in a mirror to facilitate the acquisition of speech–reading skills." (p. 25).

Johann Conrad Ammann did not enjoy such a long life. According to all available and reliable sources he passed away in 1724.

HELEN LANE

The History of Central Institute for the Deaf. St Louis/Missouri 1981.

1.   "(...) Dr Goldstein displayed his collection of old and rare books. Those that received special attention and publicity were (...) 'Oral Methods for the Deaf' by Samuel Heinicke, a Lutheran pastor, written in 1737. (...)." (p. 38).

Samuel Heinicke (1727–1790) studied, when he was already 30 years old, philosophy, mathematics and science at the university of Jena. Later on, he was sacristan and teacher at Eppendorf near Hamburg. There and then at Leipzig the instruction of deaf children became his life work. At no time of his life did Heinicke study theology and he was also never a Lutheran pastor. And because he was a boy of only ten years of age in 1737, he hardly can be the author of the book mentioned by Helen Lane.

The old and rare book which Dr Max Goldstein (1870–1941) will perhaps have acquired during the years which he had spent together with Dr Viktor Urbantschitsch in Vienna, could be a book written by Johann Ludwig Ferdinand Arnoldi. Arnoldi was born in 1737, studied theology at Giessen and was a Protestant pastor at Grosslinden near Giessen from 1768 till his death in 1783. Arnoldi is the author of the following book: "Praktische Unterweisung Taubstumme Personen reden und Schreiben zu lehren" (1777) (=Practical instruction how to teach deaf-mute person to speak and to write).

ANDREAS MARKIDES

The Use of Residual Hearing in the Education of Hearing–Impaired Children – A Historical Perspective. In: The Volta Review, 88 (5/1986), p. 57–66.

1.   "Principally involved were Pedro Ponce de León (1529–1584), Manuel Ramirez de Carrión (1579–1652), and Juan Pablo Bonet (1570–1629)." (p. 58).

Markides states also in his contribution on "the teaching of speech: historical developments" (1983) that the term of life of Pedro Ponce de León lasted from 1529 till 1584. This would mean that he had reached only an age of 55 years, although Markides remarks in the same contribution that "Pedro Ponce lives to a good old age (...)." (p. 7).

Incorrect are the dates of life of Pedro Ponce de León as well as of Juan Pablo Bonet.

Pedro Ponce de León:

There is no doubt that Pedro Ponce de León passed away on the 29th of August of 1584. There are, however, different dates about the year of his birth. Ernst Emmerig (1927, p. 16) quotes the year 1508. Hans Werner, who had a profound knowledge about the beginningsof the education of deaf children in Spain, proceeds on the assumption that Pedro Ponce "born at the beginning of the century, has made his monastic vow (...) on the 3rd of November of 1526" (1932, p. 142). This means that he cannot be born as late as 1520, as it is stated – among others – by Ruth Bender. And by no means can he be born as late as 1529. Paul Schumann was also aware of the uncertainty about the date of birth of Pedro Ponce de León. He writes: "Date and place of birth are unknown. He made his monastic vow on the 3rd of November of 1526 (...) and moved before the year 1540, not yet 30 years old, to the monastery of San Salvador at Oña, where de died on the 29th of August of 1584." (1940, p. 42).

If we can trust a newer Spanish Notice, Pedro Ponce de León was born in the year of 1510 (Perello 1977, P. 801).

Juan Pablo Bonet:

He did not live from 1570 till 1629, but from 1579 till 1633, as Hans Werner could document. (1932, p. 205 and 215).

2.   "The first professional to use the residual hearing of deaf children was a French audiologist, Jean Gaspard Marie Itard (1775–1838). (p. 59).

I leave it undecided whether one can call Itard an "audiologist" at that point in history. He studied medicine and acted as a surgeon from 1796. Since 1801 he was school medical officer at the school for the deaf in Paris which was founded by Abbe de l'Epee in 1760. Itard is regarded as one of the first ENT doctors. Also Emmerig states that his year of birth was 1775. Very probably he was born one year earlier. Mittelstädt gives the following dates of Itard's life; "Itard, Jan Marc–Gaspard (24.4.1774 Oraisson, Basses–Alpes–5.7.1838 Beau–Sejour, Passy)." (p. 1560).

3.   "Amman was a medical man from Switzerland who later on, because of religious persecution, settled in Holland." (p. 11).

It has not been possible to find a single source to confirm the statement that Ammann had suffered from religious persecution in Switzerland. On the contrary, it is known that he had received a call from his home–town Schaffhausen which had offered him an appointment. He did, however, not accept it, but visited his native town once more only a few months before he died (at Warmond near Leiden in the Netherlands).

It is possible that Markides mistook Ammann for Henry Daniel Guyot (1753–1828) whose family had to emigrate to religious reasons and found asylum in the Netherlands. The Guyots did, however, not come from Switzerland; they were Huguenots from France.

4.   "Friedrich Moritz Hill (...) studied under the famous Heinrich Pestalozzi." (Markides 1983, p. 17).

A similar sentence like this one can be found in the already mentioned book of Ruth Bender (1981, p. 126). Hill was, however, never trained by Johann Heinrich Pestalozzi, he never had studied under him, but he was trained by teachers "of whom some were direct disciples of Pestalozzi and who exercised a strong influence on him through their example and their teaching." (Schumann 1940, p. 305).

M G McLOUGHLIN

History of the Education of the Deaf in England. Liverpool 1987.

1.   "Juan Martin Bonet (born 1579) wrote the 'Simplification of Sounds and the Art of Teaching the Dumb to Speak' (1620)." (p. 1).

Juan Pablo Bonet was also given the christian name Martin, as Hans Werner (1932, p. 203) could document, but he called himself always only Juan Pablo; thus also on the title-page of his book "Reducción de las letra y arte para ensenar a ablar los mudos." M G McLoughlin did not translate this title in a correct way. The equivalent English word for the Spanish "letra" is "letter" and not "sound".

2.   "The French Institution, founded by the Abbe de l'Epee (1712–1789) in Paris with royal funds from a disused convent (...)." (p. 2).

This sentence can – according to the wording – only be understood in that way that the school for deaf children, which was founded by Abbe de l'Epee in Paris in 1760, was financially supported from its beginning by royal funds. This was, however, not the case: "Not till 1785 did he (=Abbe de l'Epee) receive an annual grant of 3400 francs out of the privy purse of Louis XVI; the government made a part of the proceeds of a dissolved convent of Coelestines and some rooms of it available to him." (Schumann 1940, p. 121–122).

EDWARD L SCOUTEN

Turning Points in the Education of Deaf People. Danville, Illinois 1984.

1.   "Ponce de León (1520–1584)." (p. 15).

This incorrect date has already been discussed.

2.   "Juan Pablo Bonet (1579–1620), ..." (p. 19).

It was already mentioned that Juan Pablo Bonet lived till 1633.

3. "Samuel Heinicke, the Father of German Oralism (1729-1790)." (p. 60).

Samuel Heinicke was born already on the 10th of April of 1727.

4. "..., Heinicke took to the road once again. It was in Hamburg that he settled and quickly set himself up as a tutor. The year was 1757. Three years later, through the assistance of some professional friends, Heinicke received an appointment as a secretary to a nobleman, one Count Schimmelmann." (p. 62).

Paul Schumann, who may be regarded as the most thorough research-worker on Samuel Heinicke, gives this information: "In 1758 he escaped abroad and settled at Altona, on Danish soil. In 1760 we find him already in Hamburg" ... where "he was occupied as tutor in the noble family of the Danish resident and treasurer Heinrich Carl Schimmelmann from 1763 till 1768." (1940, p. 146).

5. " ..., young Hill was accepted as student by the renowned Pestalozzi at his normal school. Upon the completion of his work with Pestalozzi, Hill was happily honoured, along with a number of other students, by being named in 1828 to Dr Graser's teacher education program at the Institution for the Deaf in Berlin. Graser's highly structured procedure for teaching deaf children quickly fired young Hill's imagination, and he became well aware that he had found his vocation." (p. 124).

It was already clarified that Hill was not a direct disciple of Pestalozzi. It was also shown – with Hill's own words – that he was far from being enthusiastic about the idea of becoming a teacher of the deaf. Here I want to mention only that Hill had received a grant for studies in Berlin in 1828. He entered, however, into the royal school for deaf children as a trainee not earlier than on the 1st of October in 1829. The director of this school was at that time not John Baptist Graser but Dr Ludwig Grasshoff (1770-1851).

CLOSING REMARKS

Many a reader of this historical essay may argue that the mentioned false statements and inferences in the quoted publications on the history of the education of hearing-impaired children are only bagatelles. There is no doubt that this is true of some of them. Nevertheless, it seems to me to be indispensable and even imperative to mention also these details, for otherwise the danger will remain that they will continue to misinform future generations of professional people.

A good knowledge of history in general and of the history of education in particular has not been in great demand during the past 25 years. The study of history can, however, contribute to avoid mistakes which were made in the past. Who is not aware of them, is doomed to repeat them. Surely one of the main purposes of a study of history is to learn from our past mistakes. The present European and – no doubt – also the present American education of deaf children offers many an example that "those who do not learn from the past are condemned to relive it." (G Santayana).

It is my view that we should ensure our details of history are correct and that as professionals we should not disregard history.

REFERENCES

ANON (n.y.). Rochester Advocate of English and Speech for the Deaf. In Memoriam Zenas Freeman Westervelt. Western New York Institution for Deaf-Mutes.

BALLANTYNE, J., and MARTIN, J.A.M. (1984). Deafness. Fourth Edition. Edinburgh/London.

BENDER, R. (1981). The Conquest of Deafness. Third Edition. Danville/Illinois.

BRILL, R. (1984). International Congresses on Education of the Deaf. An Analytical History 1878-1980. Washington, D.C.

BURCHETT, J. (1964). Utmost for the Highest. The Story of the Victorian School for Deaf Children.

DALE, D.M.C. (1984). Individualised Integration – Studies of Deaf and Partially-hearing Children and Students in Ordinary Schools and Colleges. London.

EMMERIG, E. (1927). Bilderatlas zur Geschichte der Taubstummenbildung. München.

EWING, A. (n.y.). History of the Department of Education of the Deaf, University of Manchester, 1919-1955. Manchester.

ERBER, N. (1982). Auditory Training. Washington D.C.

FRENCH-ST GEORGE, M., and STOKER, R (1988). Speechreading: An International Perspective In: The Volta Review, 90 (5/1988), 17-31.

HEESE, G., and WEGENER, H. (Hrsg.) (1969). Enzyklopädisches Handbuch der Sonderpädagogik und ihrer Grenzgebiete. Berlin.

KARTH, J. (Hrsg.) (1902). Das Taubstummenwesen im XIX. Jahrhundert in den wichtigsten Staaten Europas. Breslau.

LANE, H. (1981). The History of the Central Institute for the Deaf. St. Louis.

LOWE, A. (1977). Die Erziehung und Bildung hörgeschädigter Kinder in der Republik Argentinien. In: hörgeschädigte kinder, 14, 143-152.

LOWE, A. (1980). Hörerziehung für hörgeschädigte Kinder: Vergangenheit-Gegenwart-Zukunft. In: Audio-Technik, Heft 31, 1-9.

LOWE, A. (1981). The historical development of oral education. In: Mulholland, A. (ed): Oral Education – Today and Tomorrow. Washington, D.C., 3-22.

LOWE, A. (1983). Gehörlosenpädagogik. In: Solarová, S. (Hrsg.): Geschichte der Sonderpädagogik. Stuttgart, 12-48.

LOWE, A. (1984). Die geschichtliche Entwicklung der Lautspracherziehung Gehörloser Kinder. In: der kinderarzt, 15, 1450-1460.

LOWE, A. (1987). Die Stellung der Gebärde im Unterricht deutscher Gehörlosenschulen. In: Uden, A, van: Gebärdensprachen von Gehörlosen und Psycholoinguistik. Heidelberg, 141–182.

LOWE, A. (1990). Errare Humanum Est. J.Brit.Ass.Teachers of the Deaf. Vol 14, No 5.

LOWE, A. (1990). Hörerziehung für hörgeschägigte Kinder Geschichte-Methoden-Möglichketen. Heidelberg.

MARKIDES, A. (1983). The Speech of Hearing-Impaired Children. Manchester.

MARKIDES, A. (1986). The Use of Residual Hearing in the Education of Hearing-Impaired Children – A Historical Perspective. In: The Volta Review, 88 (5/1986), 57–66.

McLOUGHLIN, M. (1987). A History of the education of the deaf in England. Liverpool.

PERELLO, J. (1977). Lexicón de Comunicología, Barcelona.

SCHUMANN, P. (1940). Geschichte des Taubstummenwesens vom deutschen Standpunkt aus dargestellt. Frankfurt/Main.

SCOUTEN, E. (1984). Turning Points in the Education of Deaf People. Danville/Illinois.

TREIBEL, E. (1881). Der zweite internationale Taubstummenlehrer-Kongress in Mailand. Berlin.

WALTHER, E. (1882). Geschichte des Taubstummenbildungswesens. Bielefeld und Leipzig.

WEDENBERG, E. (1954). Auditory Training of severely hard of hearing pre-school children. In: Reprint from Acta Oto-Laryngolica, Supplementum 110, 9–82.

WERNER, H. (1932). Geschichte des Taubstummenproblems bis ins 17. Jahrhundert. Jena.

WOLLERMAN, R.O., und E. (1912). Quellenbuch zur Geschichte und Methodik des Taubstummenunterrichts. Band 2. Stettin.

The Essence of Tommy
by
Arthur Dimmock

On a chilly October day in 1958 an unposh car went along Fulham Road, Chelsea, London's artist quarters and turned into Fernshaw Road. It pulled up outside Milton House, a large old building that was a former sanctuary for unmarried mothers. The driver got out, went round and opened a door to let out a young woman of small stature. She was clad in a coat that appeared well worn and a headscarf covered her head. She carried a small attache case. A patrolling policeman, alerted in advance, on the opposite side of the road saw the woman climb the few steps leading to the large door. She paused to look at the several bell-pushes and noticed the name of the person she was to contact. She rang, the door opened and she was ushered in. Next she entered a ground floor studio and approached a man, obviously an artist, whose two-metre height towered over her. He bowed slightly and his wife at his side curtsied. The caller was Elizabeth, Queen of United Kingdom and dominions overseas. She removed her coat to reveal a V-necked dress with a royal blue ribbon running diagonally across her chest. From her case she removed a tiara and necklace, clear imitation and placed them where appropriate. She sat down and the artist, A R Thomson, RA, commenced to work on a large canvas that seemed to occupy most of the studio space. His wife chatted with the Queen to keep her from getting bored. Thomson was doing a painting of a banquet presided by the Queen. At her side in the picture was her husband, Prince Philip, in the uniform of an air force commander. Surrounding the couple were dignitaries of the air force. This picture was commissioned by the Royal Air Force to commemorate its 40th anniversary of its taking over of the Royal Flying Corps.

Alfred Reginald Thomson was born at Bangalore, Mysore, in India in 1894. His father was an inland revenue paymaster for the British army stationed there and held the rank of major. An army doctor pronounced Alfred born deaf when he failed to respond to his father's callings. During early boyhood he developed a liking for drawing figures, mostly animals, on the white walls that surrounded the family house. The father, George Thomson, came to England to choose a school for his son. The following year, 1901, father, mother and son sailed for England in the Australis which had been sunk, raised and restored to its former glory. A tearful scene ensued when the parents departed leaving the youngster in the strange atmosphere of the Margate School for the Deaf. He never saw his mother again. She died soon after her return to India, reputed from grief. Alfred grew into a tall and frequently sick boy. His school record was undistinguished but he showed some promise in art. When asked by a teacher what he wanted as an occupation when he left school, he mentioned artist.

"Artist", retorted the teacher, "this is madness. Who wants pictures?" His father on leave was dismayed at his poor school attainment and notable absence of speech so he had the boy removed to the Barber Oral School in North London. From this school he acquired nothing but unintelligible speech. Fortunately on the advice of Miss Burge, his art teacher at Margate, he was allowed to attend an art school in Central London. His tutor was the son of Sir William Orchardson, a leading artist at that time. George Thomson on hearing of his son's involvement in art was furious. He came over from India and forced him into a farm in Kent as a fee paying agricultural student. Instead of being trained he was made to work like a slave and was forbidden to have anything connected with art like paper, pencil or paint. He endured this harsh existence for two years before fleeing to Chelsea in London. In 1916 he set himself up as an artist in Redfern Road, known as the "Road of Hopefuls". As a result his father disowned him. He sat for the entrance examination for the Royal Academy School of Art but he failed and this made him think seriously about his future. He took up farming, this time working for a pleasant woman farmer in Bedfordshire but it was short lived. The lure of art was far too strong and he rushed back to Chelsea. He did paintings for a mere pittance and soon became destitute, often going without food for days and sleeping in the vaults of St Martins in the Field church which was used to shelter the homeless. The break came when he was befriended by a wealthy woman whom he met at an all-night club. She fed and housed him for a time. His forenames were distasteful to her so she christened him "Tommy" and henceforth he became known by this appellation to his contemporaries. Her influence enabled Thomson to obtain work as a commercial artist. His drawings for advertising Daimler cars and Tuborg beer became famous later. A sympathetic architect commissioned him to do murals for the walls of Duncannon, a well known central London public house. Its four walls displayed Dickensian characters in their relevant environments. These paintings made an impact in the art world and were mentioned in the press more than once. This made him known and he was accepted as a member of the elite Chelsea Arts Club but with some reluctance owing to his deafness. He became friendly with fellow members, Augustus John and Sir William Orpen, who were artists of great renown. John found Thomson a teaching post in East London. He taught by written notes and correcting details on students' works. He was made welcome at John's villa at Martigue in South France and he went several times. While there he was given work to do murals at a nearby house of a wealthy family. Life became less harsh as his reputation was established.

In 1938, Essex County Council proclaimed an open competition for a painting relating to the Pilgrim Fathers who were mostly of Essex origin. After spending several days at Plymouth where the Pilgrim Fathers embarked for American and studying historical records at the British Museum, Thomson sent an entry. After judging the short list was whittled down to four which included two Royal Academicians and Thomson. In the final round he was declared the outright winner. His painting showing an embarkment scene was hung on the Royal Wall at the following Summer Exhibition of the Royal Academy. The press and critics gave it an overwhelming acclaim and Thomson was immediately elated to the status of Associate of the Royal Academy. His ambition was fulfilled and his mind was brought back to the teacher who said "Who wants pictures?" His father, now retired, made no attempt to recognise his son's astronomical success. Thomson's future was assured.

Famous people took turns to be painted by the now famous deaf and dumb artist. During the second world war he served as the official Royal Air Force artist and while at an airfield he failed to hear the challenge of a sentry who shot him in the shoulder. The bullet remained there as its removal would have paralysed his arm. After the war he became a senior academician and served on the hanging committee for six years. He disliked the position as it means rejecting the works of so many aspiring artists. Thomson was the first man in history to be allowed to paint the interiors of the Houses of Commons and Lords. He turned out paintings of both houses in session and this involved visits to his studio of many famous people of the realm including Churchill, Atlee, Macmillan and others. These two large pictures branded him as one of the greatest specialists in the difficult art of composite groups. His "Seated Boxer" won him a gold medal in the art section of the London Olympics in 1948. Dogged by ill health he continued to work till the last few days before he died at the age of 84 in 1979.

His works can be founded in many art galleries in the world. The Queen herself owns about a dozen of his pictures. His first marriage in 1927 was a disaster but in 1940 he made Gertrude Parker his second wife and they were wonderfully happy. They had two children. Both wives acted as his manager, secretary and mouthpiece.

This then is a genius in a nutshell whose life I have recorded in detail as an example to all those deaf people to avoid accepting the discouragement of all those oralist teachers, parents and anyone else who fosters the defeatist "Deaf Can't" lie.

I hope you all get the message "Deaf Can".

Deaf Body Language frozen in Time:
Detail from the Duncannon Murals
by A R Thomson, RA, RP, RBA
(1894–1979)

On Seeing Garrick Act

by
Charles Sheriff

When Britain's Roscius on the stage appears,
Who charms all eyes, and (I am told) all ears,
With ease the various passions I can trace,
Clearly reflect'd from that wond'rous face;
Whilst true conception with just action joined,
Strongly impress each image on my mind: –
What needs of sounds when I plainly decry
The expressive features, and the speaking eye?
That eye who bright and penetrating ray
Doth Shakespeare's meaning to my soul convey:
Best commentator on great Shakespeare's text!
When Garrick acts, no passage seems perplext.

This poem by the first pupil of Braidwood's Academy in Edinburgh was published in 1768 and subsequently appeared in many journals and periodicals, mostly hitherto unaware that deaf children could be educated to such a level of creative fluency in written language.

My Rainbow, My World
(written for the Gallaudet Touring Theatre's production of "HOW")
by
Willard J Madsen – 1978

You know I'm deaf; my ears, they do not hear;
And yet I neither cry nor do I fear.
I see, I feel, I smell, I even touch,
And let my hands create the world as such
As mind perceives; it does not matter much.

You see a rainbow now before your eyes;
Some birds in flight, some brilliant butterflies,
And shining lakes or mountains far away,
And puffy clouds of white and deer at play;
And this is what my hands do everyday.

You see the world is one large orchestra
A constant melody that sets us free;
And, if I choose, I can by some design
Create a marvelous world that's all mind,
And do it with this language we call SIGN!

Do you see the rainbow in the sky?
Do you ever wonder, "Can I fly?"
And if you could, would you like to go
And sit atop the arch of a rainbow,
And view the whole wide world down below?

Or sit, perhaps, upon a grassy hill
And marvel at its colors if you will;
The brilliant yellow, orange, and red or blue
And purple fantasy or bright green hue,
With birds and butterflies as free as you!

from: A Holythroat Symposium
by
Aaron Williamson

*The spatial realm of the silence is
a parchment of skin rolled thinly into a
weapon. From the threatened unrolling
of its disfigured surface comes
obeisance. Incisions and curses.
Deplorable, unspeakable tempers bark
loose from its veneer into the chasmic
hush. An echo-sounder would verify an
upright tunnel but the sullen menace of
quiescence must not be probed. Within,
a figure has chosen to occupy an
unexceptional area. It moves
infrequently, each time to cast a face
at some imagined or unverified
companion. Obscure in meaning and
intention, these attitudes of visage
are thrown, held briefly, and collapsed
at metronomic intervals. Gradually,
this catalogue of humours, at first
wildly capricious, begins to seem
connected. A residue of feedback is
framing up the mind. The tempo is
driven forward. Mugging frantically
with grimaces and frowns, the movements
begin to diminish: spasms to twitches,
small flickerings around the eyes.
Concurrent with this abatement in
volume, the transformations are
accelerated and the face appears to
move towards its optimum portrayal.
This will be an enigma. The final swift
and minute adjustments are
heartbreaking: so much so that we no
longer wish to observe. There is
something untouchable and yes,
preposterous here. Petrifying. Indeed,
we are captive, stricken in its stare.
Our fear preserved and confirms its
secret and isolation creeps in from
the loss of antennae; from the loss,
that is, of our response. Out of the
deadlock, the distance sense is spun
amok. We are going it alone. No means
by which to monitor this thought and
feeling. Within the silence, head to
head, the ear is our mirror.*

INTERROBANG THE BRAKE

citation:
(breathe here)
but for the sake of
densification
and since the passional ambidextres
are unknown...
ADPRESS THE SYZYGY
its synechdoche
– dystrophy –
& pushing upon tresses
curlycueing with diphthongs
rasping
at the seraphim intake
(breathe here again)
AN OVERHANG OF SPAKE
cascading hirsute
commencement
significant in measure
meant:
HARANGUE ITS ACHE
chimeric crank underhand
echoic refund
of REMANENT
a FAKE
reMAKE
...swilled under this jaw–clamp
I–said–swilling
(the sheer phonetic drive
of an ever–deepening
pocket of sense:
posterity, particularly,
is always trying to catch up...)
on the GIBSTAFF
angle–cantilevered signalflake
in the CAN CAN of a CORNCRAKE
...in the sounding of a bradawl
placed gently in contact with a denture's glint
– waiting –
(until)
you SAID IT

sssssssssssssssssssss

Appendum

The central design
in conducting 'A Holythroat Symposium'
was to fortify the conjunction
between
a sense of identity
evolving from out of the physical situation
or 'hors de combat'
of deafness
and the ongoing exertion
and problem
of engendering texts.
That is,
to oscillate between
what has become congested
into a state of anatomy
and the mechanical synopsis of its trace
thereby
diminishing the distance
of its seesawing
to this end.

The primary source of identification
the body
as residue
conducting fulgurative interrogations
of the phonic
in and around language
yet to one side of its drag.

Or: I am nervous about life
the irrigation of its dreaming
cataclinal
yet never ceasing
with the pooling of itself
amounting to these cries:
these cries which are also
invaginations
at the tip of a stiletto.

First, the title.
I wanted to suggest
the sanctity of vocalisation
as anatomical process
within an environment
that is usually normalising it
into an activity which is granted.
By proposing a 'holiness'
to speech
the work may begin to imitate
an archaic convention
of ascribing anatomical residence
for god

as being inside the voice:
a voice which is not only
the voice of its speech.
The throat
in its turn
suggests a physiognomy
a concrete metonymic specification
– the block on which this threnody
is measured off –
'throttled out of its thrombotic thoroughfare'

Symposium:
initially
a meeting of people
for the purpose of inebriation
– a hidden flaw
subsiding liabilities
in upholding myths
(talking activities) –
around forms
whilst contemplating an ideological status
for a specific one:
the body of work as it
pulls at its ballast.

The writing then, addresses issues
which, overlapping,
are stated repeatedly
– failing in a sense, its oto-reception –
repeatedly
from out of separate soundsource or contexts:
a holythroat symposium.

From: A Holythroat Symposium
        Creation Books, 1993
        83 Clerkenwell Road
        London

ACADEMIC AND MEDIA LANGUAGE

"Oh ye tak the high road,
and I'll tak the low road..."

for Bill Stokoe
by
Mervin Garretson

in other years our light burned low
o darkest night
sign hung up on the cross
verboten was the word
deaf as a culture lost
nothing we saw was heard

gone days of Milan smog
careening in the fog
clods in a world of sound
clouds in a cloudless sky
mouthing like jesters crowned
questing the untold why

of life just one small part
a shadow of the whole
sign buried in the heart
language without a soul.

somewhere a lighthouse gleam
someone who dared to dream
a candle lit, a flame
soaring from mind to hand
that swept across our land

what's in this man, a cause
that seeks the are, not was
transfiguring night to day

with every newfound rule
facing the angry sway
of time and ridicule

we'll not forget the hour
he came to Gallaudet
the sun shone hope
the smog glowed stars

At The Beach
by
Willard J Madsen

The calm of the ocean
A wave that's unheard
And sparkling sandstones –
Swift flight of a bird.
On the beach below me
Lie a multitude
Of bodies and blankets,
And umbrellas protrude
From the waves of the sand.

On distant horizon
A ship sailing by –
And red flags waving
Where surf meets the sky.
A lifeguard's still signals
Send messages far
Up and down the beachhead
Do you know what they are?

Wish I could decipher
And know what they say,
But I only wonder
As a dreamer may –
Not knowing the language
Of the ships at sea,
Of sailors and lifeguards,
Whatever it be.

And I wonder if others
Who watch you and me
Might share the same feeling
When they see us use Sign –
A language that clearly
Is yours and is mine!

Language for the Brain

a personal view of Sign Language in the development of Deaf Education in Britain
by
Murray Holmes
Chairman of the British Deaf Association

"Communication should begin in the
cradle and a mother or a nurse
should have as nimble a hand
as commonly they have a tongue"

George Dalgarno, Aberdeen, Scotland 1661

In 1940, the British army pulled out of Dunkirk in disarray and a victorious fascist regime settled down to impose their 'NEW ORDER' on Europe for, what they fondly hoped, all time. The Deaf Dunkirk was 60 years earlier, at the 'Congress of Milan' in 1880. Here the defeat was of commonsense, when the largely hearing assembly voted by a small majority to educate Deaf children by the oral method and to ban the use of the Language of signs and fingerspelling in the classroom.

Previous to this, the use of manual methods had meant that there was a place for Deaf teachers in education, but after 'Milan' this ceased to be common and some schools even sacked Deaf teachers there and then. Their dismissal was on the grounds of educational theory, as rigidly dogmatic as any purge of political dissidents in a totalitarian regime.

Over the past century, the effects of the Milan Resolution have bitten deep into the life of Deaf children and has corroded the very structure of Deaf society. The most obvious effect of the oral only approach to education was to deprive thousands of Deaf children of the basic education necessary to exercise their full rights as citizens. As one of the victims, I was denied access to ordinary information about life in general, until I left school, and mercifully gained access via a manual language at technical college. (Holmes 1980).

Thus I am not talking about history when I talk of the Milan Congress, and refresh your memories only to show how an unimaginative majority can enforce a monumental and lasting injustice on a minority. This kind of injustice is relatively easy to avoid if the minority are properly represented in the decision-making groups which influence their future. When the minority is the sole consumer as in Deaf education, then the argument from excluding them is not only unjust, but impractical, not only undemocratic but arbitrary to the point of stupidity. In the management of all institutions and organisations for Deaf people, a deaf presence on governing bodies, both legislative and executive, along the lines suggested by the 1980 Warnock report, would improve conditions for the consumer.

To understand the tragic effects the Milan Resolution imposed on the British Deaf community, it is necessary to examine the growth of Sign Language and Deaf Education, right from the start.

From time immemorial, Sign Language has been used by Deaf communities worldwide. Reference to Sign Language can be found in the Bible. It is realistic to assume that the development of Sign Language runs parallel with spoken language. If we go back in time to Neanderthal Man we will find that Sign Language originated before spoken language. The earliest written record of Sign used in Britain can be traced to the Venerable Bede's Chronicles, written around 685 AD and states that St John of Beverley ministered to the needs of Deaf youths and devised a two handed alphabet system based on market place number signs. It can be claimed that St John of Beverley was the world's first teacher of the Deaf, that is why so many institutions and schools in Britain regard him as the Patron Saint of the Deaf.

History and folklore tell us that prior to the establishment of schools for the Deaf in Britain and Europe, most deaf people were uneducated, incompetent, simple minded and leading lives of isolation within their own communities. (Jackson 1990). This assertion is probably correct for some deaf people in distant times as there are still some simple minded incompetent deaf people in the 1990's. Unless they came from wealthy families, very few hearing people received schooling in distant times and there were numerous incompetent, simple minded hearing people as there are today. Therefore classification in this case is meaningless.

Sign Language is a visual language and does not have a long history unless it is written about or painted, or built as a permanent structure, and herein lies the greatest difficulty in looking at the history of British Sign Language. Thus we rely on the writings of hearing people to give us the factual history of Sign Language. The earliest writings related to Sign Language are found in the Hebrew book of Talmud and the Christian Bible. The earliest writings about Sign Language in this country, apart from St Bede's Chronicles, emerge in Richard Carew's 'Survey of Cornwall', published in 1595 and John Bulwer's 'Deaf and Dumb Man's Friend', published in 1648.

In Richard Carew's 'A Survey of Cornwall', a full page is devoted to Edward Bone, a Deaf and Dumb manservant of Peter Courtney who was a Member of Parliament for Cornwall. Bone had excellent lipreading facilities and is described in the book as attending public meetings, focusing on the speakers, then returning to his master to report, verbatim, what was said at the meeting. He used Sign Language to communicate with his master, who was also fluent in Sign Language. It is written that Bone was unable to speak. He had a retarded deaf brother, so it is assumed his deafness was hereditary. This is the first independent observation in Britain of how a Deaf person could lipread and communicate with his hearing employer by signs and seek out other Deaf persons and communicate in a Sign Language, not readily understood by most hearing people at that time.

John Bulwer mentioned in his book, the existence of over 25 Deaf persons in various parts of the country, mostly in London, Essex and the South East who communicated in Sign Language. Bulwer makes a dedication to Sir Edward Getwick, who was a hearing and a fluent user of Sign Language, was a regular traveller and it was probably him who gave Bulwer the names of Deaf persons mentioned in the book.

The diarist Samuel Pepys, in his account about The Great Fire written in 1666, mentions the story told by George Downing from Maidstone, Kent, about the observations of the fire, related by a Deaf and Dumb boy in strange signs and gestures. These strange signs and gestures were in fact British Sign Language, of which Downing was fluent and could interpret into spoken language. It is a fact that the first settlers to Martha's Vineyard in USA came from Kent, which led to British Sign Language being used by the large Deaf community on Martha's Vineyard for centuries.

There is no exact history as to who invented the two handed fingerspelling which is described in the works of George Dalgarno of Aberdeen. Perhaps it was a derivation from the system devised by St John of Beverley and reproducibly described by St Bede. Before the onset of Deaf education, most of Europe used the two handed fingerspelling system. This is supported by the painting 'The Master and Pupil' by the Flemish artist Jacob de Gheyn 1599 which clearly illustrates the two handed system. On a visit to Bulgaria in 1979, the author was told by Deaf people in that country, two handed fingerspelling was used right up to 1935. Also he was able to observe elderly Deaf people using signs based on the two handed version, incorporating the Cyrillic finger alphabet.

We have now established that there existed a system of Sign Language and fingerspelling, which had its own grammar and structure around 1630, and was most likely used by Deaf and some hearing people for centuries before that date. Historical record shows us that King James I and VI tried to establish a Professor of Signs. All this happened before the onset of Deaf Education in the middle of the 18th Century.

The exact origin of Deaf Education is shrouded in controversy, with various countries and individuals claiming to be the first to teach the Deaf. As mentioned earlier, the Venerable Bede's Chronicles give us the earliest written attempts to give the Deaf an education. Since that time, undoubtedly, many unrecorded instances had been made by various individuals in Europe, to impart education to the Deaf, by both oral and manual means.

The first written record that can be traced, since St Bede's Chronicles, is of the Spanish Monk, Pedro Ponce de Leon, who taught the Deaf by Sign Language and later by an oralist system, at the monastery of San Salvador in Ona, Spain in the later part of the 16th Century. John Wallis, a founding member of the Royal Society and Professor of Geometry at Oxford is credited as being the first Briton to teach by the oralist method after first using Sign Language, adopted from the Spanish system around 1680. Also in 1680, George Dalgarno published an account on teaching the Deaf by Sign Language, although there is no record of him actually using the system to teach the Deaf.

During the ensuing 100 years, there is record of various Deaf individuals achieving academic fame. These individuals were mostly the offspring of wealthy and influential families who could afford private tuition. It wasn't until the second half of the 18th Century, that Le'Epée in France, Heinicke in Germany and Braidwood in Britain opened the door to public education for the Deaf. Heinicke used the oral only method and both Le'Epée and Braidwood adopted Sign Language as the teaching medium although Braidwood, later, publically professed oralism.

In 1760, Thomas Braidwood, owner of a small private school in Edinburgh, was approached by a wealthy merchant and asked to educate his Deaf and Dumb son. Thus, from a small beginning, Braidwood opened the first school in Britain for the Deaf. It was known as Braidwood's Academy and catered for children, mostly from wealthy families but also took on poor Deaf children. Braidwood taught by fingerspelling and sign whilst his school was in Edinburgh. Many of his pupils went on to make remarkable achievements. One notable pupil was John Goodricke the astronomer, who is credited with the discovery of the star Algol. John Goodricke had no understandable speech and communicated by fingerspelling, sign and writing.

In 1783, Braidwood moved his Academy to Hackney, London and later converted to the oralist only method of teaching the Deaf. This tradition was carried out by other members of his family and his grandson, used it at his school in the USA. It is worth mentioning here that after Thomas Braidwood's death in 1806, Thomas Hopkins Gallaudet, the American fire and brimstone preacher, arrived in England in 1815 asking to be given the Braidwood 'secret' of teaching the Deaf and Dumb. This was refused by Robert Kinniburgh, an evangelical minister who had succeeded Braidwood as Headmaster at the Hackney school. Gallaudet then turned to Abbé Sicard, who had succeeded Lépée at the Paris School for the Deaf and Mute. Sicard welcomed him with open arms and to this day the one handed manual alphabet is widespread in the USA.

As we can see, the earliest provision of education for the Deaf was available only to the wealthy. No actual provision was made for the poor Deaf until a period of philanthropy at the turn of the 19th Century. Between 1800 and 1850, 15 schools were established and many grew into great residential institutions with hundreds of Deaf pupils and employing both Deaf and hearing teachers. Many of these institutions are still with us today, to name a few we have Margate School, Yorkshire Residential School at Doncaster, Donaldson's in Edinburgh, Northern Counties at Newcastle, Royal Exeter School and Elmet Hall in Leeds.

These schools used sign and two handed fingerspelling to educate the Deaf children in their care. The school environment was normal as both children and teacher could converse at ease with each other. Deaf culture and history was passed from one generation to the next. The children left school with adequate language and writing skills to enable them to fit into society with considerable ease. Employment was mostly to be obtained by the craft trades such as shoemaking, carpentry, tailoring and printing for the boys, dressmaking, laundry work and as domestic helps for the girls. The same sort of work was generally available to hearing contemporaries at that time, although the exceptionally academic Deaf entered the teaching profession as Deaf Teachers of the Deaf, a title of which they were exceedingly proud to have. This period was referred to by the older Deaf, whom I was privileged to meet in the mid 1950's, as the 'Deaf Utopia' continued right up to the 'Milan Resolution'.

The effects of the Milan Resolution, which was later endorsed by a Royal Commission Report in 1889, did not happen immediately. Hearing teachers had to be trained in the new oralist method (I am not aware of any Deaf teacher being trained in this method). In fact there were still Deaf teachers right up to the early stage of World War 2. This along with the fact there were still hearing teachers around, who understood the importance of Sign Language in the Deaf child's educational development and used it in the dormitories, after school hours, ensured that the Deaf pupils, at that time, had adequate understanding of life skills and were prepared for the world of work. (Holmes 1990).

In the aftermath of the horrors of the Great War (1914–1918) people were desperate to make society a better place in which to live. The noble dream of making the dumb to speak was the main attraction to the new breed of teachers entering Deaf education as oralist teachers at that time. There is evidence that between the two world wars, Deaf children in the residential schools received a mixture of oralism and Sign Language as their educational diet. t depended on who was the class teacher at that time, one of the new breed of Manchester trained oralists or one of the old brigade who professed to have converted to oralism in order to safeguard their jobs, but in reality practised Sign Language.

It was at the end of the last war and early 1950's that 'Oralism Milan Style' began to make a tragic and lasting effect on the Deaf community. Without the benefit of having Sign Language passed down through the generation grapevine, Deaf school leavers turned up at the local Deaf Clubs unable to make normal conversation with their peers who were fluent signers. Because of their lack of life skills and behaviourial problems, social workers were finding it increasingly difficult to find gainful employment for them. This was most evident with pupils from the small oralist schools that had sprung up since 1890. (Holmes 1990).

I quote my own experience, having attended one such school in Paisley. The school consisted of some 20 pupils, with varying degrees of deafness, between the ages of 3 to 16. The classes were split by age and no matter how intelligent an individual child may have been, he was made to stay with his own age group, even if it meant lagging behind educationally. A typical school day began with morning reading, writing and the all important, time consuming speech therapy using amplified group hearing aids, regardless of the severity of one's deafness. Afternoons were set apart for basic arithmetic and other subjects such as art and history, but always with the inevitable aids for speech training. In my own estimate, I judge that about 40% of my time at school was spent on speech training and lipreading. The reason given for this unbalanced educational diet was that they believed it would normalise the child and make him fit into the hearing world with utmost ease. (Holmes 1980).

The school climate was far from normal. In a town of 90,000 there was an insufficient number of Deaf pupils to ensure a representative group of normally Deaf children and as the age groups fluctuated according to the incidence fashions of deafness, one's classmates depended on chance not proper classification. How does one enjoy a normal harmonious school environment when even the age range of the class depends on chance. I became the oldest boy in the school at 13 years and suffered a further 3 years of indignity and injustice by having no playmate of my own age, the nearest being 4 years my junior. (Holmes 1980).

I left school at the age of 16 with no academic qualifications whatsoever. However, I excelled at metalwork and was able to obtain employment in the engineering industry as an apprentice toolmaker. One of the conditions of my apprenticeship was that I attend day release classes. Day release was a special class for Deaf students at a college of engineering in Glasgow where one or two of the technical teachers had been taught fingerspelling and a few rudimentary signs. These teachers had no formal training as teachers of the Deaf, therefore were unaware of 'Oralism Milan'. They adopted the communication method as given to them by the Deaf students. Within months, I advanced from basic arithmetic to mathematics and mastered the problems of engineering science and technology. I gained more knowledge in my 5 years at day release than the entire time I spent at the school for the Deaf. There was no speech therapy or lipreading to hinder my educational progress, just fingerspelling and written data on the blackboard. I completed the course with a full certificate in Mechanical Engineering Technology and due to this experience, was further encouraged to study for the GCE in English, English Literature and Mathematics, which I duly passed via a correspondence course.

It was at this point in my career that I began to wonder why I had to wait so long for an effective communication method to give me access to the entire world of education, now opened up to me. What was the aim of education of the Deaf? Was it primarily to make us as 'normal as possible' in speech only or should a broader approach to language (not simply speech) leading to a more normal general education be the aim? I am inclined to agree with George Montgomery's paper which claims that many authorities responsible for deaf education are more concerned with defective ears than effective brains. There are many parts of the brain in need of stimulation, other than speech areas and Sign Language refreshes the parts that oralism cannot reach. (Montgomery 1979).

The oralist idea that spoken words are necessary to think with was the main fallacy which led to the prohibition of manual language. From a Deaf viewpoint, ample everyday evidence of thought without spoken language suggests that this fallacy is hard to beat for sheer lack of commonsense. (Holmes 1980).

Fortunately for us, during the last decade the new influx of teachers of the Deaf have, at last, acknowledged the fact put forward by Deaf adults for the past 100 years, that Sign Language is a vital and necessary ingredient which will stimulate the educational progress of the Deaf School child. This acceptance was made possible by the pioneering research and evidence submitted by Conrad, Vernon, Montgomery and others. This research has endorsed the view advocated by the Deaf community since day 1 from the infamous Milan Resolution.

Since 1984, Teachers of the Deaf have accepted Signed English, Sign Language and fingerspelling as official methods to be used by those schools that choose to use them. Some schools have enthusiastically adopted Total Communication or some form of bilingual teaching and the recruitment of Deaf staff has improved. Other teachers, in some parts of the country, however, still have misgivings as to the benefit of a method of communication that is both alien and pantomime to them. Without having any in depth understanding of the language, they state it is ungrammatical and therefore unacceptable in the acquisition of the all important spoken English.

The view that Sign Language is ungrammatical is utter nonsense. It is a typical view held by a stubbornly conformist group who are inclined to hold fast the doctrine and techniques acquired at Teaching Training College. (Montgomery 1979).

Language must be introduced and acquired as early as possible or its development may be permanently retarded and impaired. This can be done with the profoundly Deaf only by Sign. Therefore deafness must be diagnosed as early as possible. Deaf children must first be exposed to fluent signers, whether these be parents, teachers or whoever. Once Signing is learnt, then all else will follow. The development of Sign grammar takes place at the same age and in the same way as the acquisition of speech grammar. (Sacks 1989). I have nearly 40 years personal experience in the Deaf community. My experience and understanding of that community is very deep indeed. I know within my own mind, it is infinitely possible by acquiring signing skills right at the start, the Deaf School child will eventually become bilingual and grammatically proficient in both Sign and written English. This is especially so if at the inception period the teacher is Deaf.

In a few units and smaller schools, Sign Language has been used right from the start and the use of Deaf support staff used to develop Language skills. Then when the child is around 7 or 8, a mainstreaming programme is implemented. This means taking the child out of special classes and integrating him in a regular class in a hearing school. This concept developed because of what is thought to be the potentially dehumanising effect of segregating groups of disabled people from the mainstream of society. The idea that disabled children should be educated in the least restrictive setting, appropriate to their needs, has achieved tremendous momentum. (Davilla 1980). The idea that the least restricting environment for a Deaf child is in the mainstream is very dubious indeed and, in practice, today the special Deaf Schools are now comprised of as many as 60% of their pupils who are refugees from inappropriate and unsuccessful mainstreaming. These children are typically several years behind in English and numeracy, those who began their education in a special school.

The situation of integration of the Deaf child in a regular class is a complex issue. It is simply not easy to accomplish integration with Deaf children as it is with children of the higher incidence disability conditions of mental retardation, learning disabilities or the physical handicapped. The situation of the Deaf child cannot be compared with that of other disabled children. Other children hear their classmates and participate in class discussions, hear the playground conversations, hear the latest gossip when moving between classes. Thesimple fact is that the Deaf child does not hear. The implications of this are self–evident and far reaching. (Garretson 1977).

The answer to all of this must, by now, be evident. What is desperately needed in this country to redress the educational imbalance of the Deaf School child is the appointment of Deaf School Teachers of the Deaf. I know there are a few already, however, we are one of the few countries in Western Europe which has no official policy to allow Deaf people to teach in schools for the Deaf.

The barrier to having Deaf Teachers in this country is the degrading, insulting and simply stupid procedure embodied in the medical rules of the General Teaching Council. Also, the British Association of Teachers of the Deaf (BATOD) have done nothing or, simply refused to do anything to remove this artificial barrier. It is within their power to recommend to the General Teaching Council that these blatant and discriminatory regulations be removed and training courses established to train Deaf people and allow them to become fully qualified and recognised Teachers for the Deaf.

The Deaf Community want to play their part in the destiny of our children, therefore, I make an impassioned appeal to BATOD to work alongside us and help to change the discriminatory rules that prevent us from attaining the accolade 'Deaf Teacher of the Deaf'. We have never said there is no place for hearing teachers of the Deaf. We acknowledge the important need for their contribution in the education of the Deaf. What we seek is a trusting partnership as teachers, which will enable Deaf children in this country to receive the best possible education. Now, when the "Total Communication" generation of Deaf children are passing regular school leaving certificates and gaining University entrance directly from special schools, it is more than ever possible to have intelligent, well-educated Deaf teachers of the Deaf and, eventually, Deaf professors at the University level as they do in Gallaudet in USA.

Five years after Dunkirk, a victorious Britain Army pushed the Nazis into history. Things move a little slower in Deaf affairs, but 114 years after Milan, the resurgence of Sign Language in education is widespread and rapidly increasing. Let us further restore Deaf people to their previous positions of responsibility, denied to them by the oralists, and fold up the oralist package, along with other repressive doctrines such as fascism, blood-letting, slavery, prohibition and other forms of human sacrifice to where they belong – in history – the Chamber of Horrors at Madame Tussauds.

References

Davilla R W (1980) Education in the Least Restrictive Environment. Proc. International Conference on Education of the Deaf, Hamburg, West Germany.

Garretson M (1977) The Hidden Curriculum in Integration & Disintegration of the Deaf in Society. SWD.

Holmes A M (1980) Milan and Me, Notes for the Biographer. SWD.

Holmes A M (1990) A Consumer's Viewpoint. SWD.

Jackson P (1990) Britain's Deaf Heritage. BDA.

Montgomery G W G (1959) Changing Attitudes to Education. BDA.

Sacks O (1990) Seeing Voices. Picador

The Academic Muse
Academic Writing for Deaf Students
by
Helen Reed

"I keep six honest serving men
They taught me all I knew
Their names are What and Why and When
And How and Where and Who"

R Kipling

While writing a dissertation for my final year BA degree at Liverpool University, I came across many challenges and surprises. As a Deaf person it was thought that doing a dissertation would be easier and more accessible than doing a three hour examination paper due to the possible English language problems in the examination room. This advantage would also enable me to research and analyse information on a longer time basis and with the aid of a dictionary! I also felt that it was important to have Deaf people to research Deaf issues to gain a deeper insight and for more understanding and positive approach. Too many hearing people have looked at deafness from a medical viewpoint and it is time for Deaf people to look at their own community from a proud and positive culture stance.

I decided to look at Deaf identity and how both Deaf and hearing people saw deafness. As I had to take a scientific approach to qualify as a psychological dissertation, I was forced to take on the hearing "way" of doing research and writing up the work. This was difficult because I can't pretend to be hearing and I can't pretend to have excellent English with knowledge of jargon in order to appear clever!! The writing of English at a high standard was difficult but necessary in order to be on equal par with my hearing peers.

Firstly I looked at what existed already on Deaf issues and I was amazed to see such a big gap – there was a huge area to be explored and not many people have researched Deafness. I was so surprised because the Deaf community is central to my life and I thought there'd be many books on Deaf culture and the Deaf aspects, such as those written by the 'Ewing' school at Manchester University. It is only in recent decades that deafness is beginning to be viewed as a cultural minority grouping and I am glad to be living in this decade to see this happening! References for my dissertation were hard to find as relevant books, articles and papers were not in my University library. This therefore meant travelling to London to visit the RNID library. Another frustration was that there were some references written in the USA, especially Gallaudet University, but it would have been too expensive to order these publications.

Secondly, I undertook both a questionnaire and a survey to ask Deaf and hearing people how they felt about deafness. It was thought that hearing people would take a traditional view of deafness in medical terms and more Deaf people would be positive in seeing their Deafness in cultural terms. But after analysing and compiling the statistical work, I was bemused to discover there was a great similarity between the views of Deaf and hearing people. Was this because those hearing people I questioned were afraid to upset me and wrote what they thought I wanted to know? As I am profoundly deaf, it is difficult to be objective and for others to treat me as a professional, and because I am an 'insider', that is, a member of the deaf community, some may say that I was too subjective and may not have seen the different way of life for Deaf people because I am used to these differences. It is important to talk with other researchers and take up lecturers' offers of advice in order to be taken seriously in your work! As I did not have the resources and the time to do the questionnaire and the survey visually, Deaf respondents may have had difficulties with the written English language as most of them would be using BSL as their preferred language. With hindsight, it would have been better to undertake the dissertation using a video camera to facilitate easier communication with Deaf respondents, but I did not have funding to do this at the time.

I have to say that Deaf students who take up the writing of a dissertation will have to expect to spend more time on it than their hearing peers because of the additional difficulties, such as analysing and researching in English and the expectations of writing of a high standard. But it is good to see more Deaf students take up this option to give themselves an advantage, with more time and more freedom in writing what they want, rather than struggling with an examination paper in a second language. It is important for Deaf students to show others, both Deaf and hearing people that Deaf people are capable of doing such things as research work – we have the insight and the understanding of our Deaf community so we need to record how the Deaf community works.

Academic Writing
Varieties of English for Students
by
George Montgomery

As the foregoing comment by Helen Reed makes clear, one of the main difficulties that deaf students experience at College and University is writing essays, reports and dissertations in English of a high standard. Sometimes writing good English is confused with using "long" words and especially contrived jargon. Good English is often clear and concise but because it has a rich vocabulary taken from Saxon, French, Latin, Greek and Scandinavian origins, inter alia, it is very common for all of us, deaf or hearing, to come across words which are not known to us. Just as in Sign Language, a good sign is often accepted into other languages eg, Japanese CHARACTERS, French PARIS, Italian MAFIA, so English is full of imported foreign words. Eg., from

Italian	pizza, paparazzi, allegro, staccato
German	blitz, flak, strudel, waltz, zeppelin
French	champagne, mutton, chagrin, oblige
Latin	senate, primary, mile, century, duke
Japanese	karaoke, kamikaze, sumo, judo, sushi
Greek	psychology, iconic, encyclopaedia, zone
Scandinavian	smorgasbord, yomp, fiord, ski, beck, dale
Gaelic	donkey, whisky, brogues, phoney, slogan
Hindi	chokka, dekko, pukka, bungalow, loot
Turkish	kiosk, harem, kebab, sultana, kismet

Bernstein claimed that there are two main varieties of English, restricted and elaborated. Academic English is mainly written in the elaborated code which may be difficult – almost foreign – to someone brought up on a restricted code.

The differences are of style, content and grammar and are usually exaggerated by limited communication approaches to the education of deaf people resulting in an English which uses short sentences, few elliptical forms, few clauses, little paragraphing, small vocabulary with much use of cliches and fixed forms and avoidance of conditionals and imaginative possibilities beyond the here and now. A further complication is that the elaborated "high class" English was developed by the rulers of England for 200 years after the Norman conquest who spoke Norman–French. Their few priests at the time who could write, wrote in Latin. Thus elaborate English has a huge vocabulary of French, Latin and Latinate words which even today have a "polite", superior tone to them – what the Americans call "40 dollar words". By contrast, words of Anglo–Saxon origin have an earthy ring to them as if suited to downtrodden peasants.

The words *guts, snot, puke, spit, dung and dead* mean exactly the same as their latinate forms *intestines, mucous, regurgitate, expectorate, manure and deceased* but the contrast between direct, forceful, blunt terms and the more genteel, polite forms is very real. It also perpetuates socially divisive and snobbish attitudes as exemplified when an enlisted private soldier reported to a medical orderly that he was wounded in the testicles. "Testicles" snorted the orderly, "only officers have testicles". This story is a reminder that some words such as the 4 letter equivalents of testicle, urinate, defecate and copulate are taboo–words used in cursing and swearing.

Thus English easily lends itself to the use of euphemism, that is polite words to disguise painful realities. The shorter forms often give offence and are often used intentionally to give offence. It is wise to avoid them in academic writing and discussion unless one is happy to be regarded as obscenely insensitive to the feelings of others. Nevertheless, the difference is sociopolitical as the referent of the words is identical. The process still goes on as the present writer has observed a bilingual Welsh mother chide her child for correctly pronouncing the guttural ch in Dolgoch in front of English speakers and "correcting" it to the incorrect Dolgoth; cf. Lock Lomond instead of Loch Lomon.

So powerfully embedded in the cultural id are the 'four letter' Saxon words that they are often better avoided or replaced with latinate equivalents. The way in which a rude joke may be cloaked by the respectability of the classical languages was demonstrated when the London Times once printed an obituary for Henry Longbottom with the quotation from Horace "Ars Longa Vita Brevis". The use of euphemistic terms as a mark of snobbish social superiority is also illustrated in the story of the rather precious Edinburgh lawyer who was asked bluntly by a Glasgow defendant "Eza Cludgie?" and replied with elegant frostiness "Just go down the stair, turn right along the corridor and you will see a door marked "GENTLEMEN". Just ignore this and go straight through."

Sometimes the incessant, compulsive use of the eff word in English is mitigated by substituting "blooming", "blinking" or "bloody". Colloquial Australian–English has adopted this latter adjective imaginatively. Although the average inhabitant of Oz doesn't give a Castlemaine XXXX for euphemism in general, a noted educationist solemnly gave the assurance that language graduates of the Victorian School for the Deaf were required to learn the following poem by heart before being admitted to Australian adulthood.

> *"Now their voices were a little loud, an' everybody heard*
> *The peculiar integration of this adjectival word.*
> *But no one there was laughin', an' me I wasn't game,*
> *So I stood around an' let 'em think I spoke the bloody*
> *same.*
> *An' one of 'em was interested to ask 'im what he'd got –*
> *How many kanga–bloody–roos he bloody went and shot –*
> *An' the shootin' bloke said, "Things are crook; the*
> *drought's too bloody tough;*
> *I got forty–bloody–seven, an' that's good e–bloody–nough.'*
> *An' this polite rejoinder seemed to satisfy the mob,*
> *An' everyone stopped listenin' an' got on with the job,*
> *Which was drinking' beer and arguin' an' talkin' of the heat,*
> *An' boggin' in the bitumen in the middle of the street;*
> *But as for me, I'm here to say the interestin' news*
> *Was 'Tumba–bloody–rumba shootin' Kanga–bloody–roos".*

Euphemism is sometimes kindly intended, sometimes akin to deceit and denial and in extreme cases, an instrument of cynical manipulation of others. Euphemism is always subject to a creditability gap which reverses its impact if it becomes too wide. Kindly intended Euphemism has long been used in medicine. "You are living with cancer – not dying of cancer." "Your son is well within the normal distribution for weight/height/intelligence." "Your wounds are healing marvellously, only two of them are fatal."

Recently, "politically correct" language has been adopted by many local and national organisations ousting insensitive language which gives offence to minorities. It is now common to avoid lumpen group terms like "The Deaf", "The Blind", "The Disabled, "The Elderly" and use instead deaf people, disabled people etc. Yet comparable terms like "The

Left", "The Scots", "Youth" (yoof), "The Mediafolk" are still acceptable to many. Also commendable is the replacement or avoidance of pejorative adjectives such as dumb, mental and crippled. Yet sometimes relabelling is not so obviously beneficial. When appealing for funding, a charity named "Cripples Aid" may be more financially successful than one named "Differently Abled Persons Support". Also, Euphemisms do not have an infinite shelf-life and are subject to a kind of linguistic inflation and devaluation. For example, the word asylum – a haven of help and sanctuary – had a noble ring to it when first applied to hospitals and institutions for the mentally and physically differenced. By constant usage, however, "asylums" came by association to have a connotation of the "total institution" described by Goffman in his classical treatise of that title.

Similarly, racial equality is usually one or two steps behind the fashionable terms for those of African origins. The word "Black" was improved to "coloured" after the abolition of slavery, then seeking the respectability of Latin, Negro was adopted. The dignity of the classics worked in Nigeria and to this very day, Nigerians are proud of their appellation. In USA however, any connection with this former slave community seems doomed and negro was declared old hat, "coloured" reinstated until it was in turn ousted by Black, then Afro-American and now African-American.

Although deaf people almost unanimously now disapprove of the linking with dumb which in German-American usage implies stupid, they are quite happy with deaf and usually wish their community to be called the Deaf (with a capital). Since the post-war medical/educational hegemony of Manchester in the study of deafness, a substantial number of workers in deafness use the term "Hearing Impaired" – one of a great many needless terms of euphemism for deafness. (Andersson Y. 1988). The label "impaired" is negative and pejorative meaning "not all there, a cracked pot, not a full deck, two chips short of a butty" or somesuch. As all of us are short of something why pick out the Deaf for a high profile impairment label? It is just as silly as calling all children "the maturity impaired", all males, "breast impaired" and until someone invents a female testicle, the list includes women also. When politically correct language is over-ambitious, the result may be counter-productive: thus whilst most accept changes such as;

deaf for deaf and dumb
slow learners for retarded, imbecile, idiot etc
senior citizens for old folk
special schools instead of the inaccurate term "segregated" schools

There is widespread hilarity over such terms as vertically challenged for tall or short follically challenged for bald and, finally, very finally, metabolically challenged for dead. A euphemism decoder is included in the jargonese section on page 164 in this volume.

Recently the editor of Silent News, who jokingly describes himself as "avoirdupoisically challenged" reported the attempt of a 360 lbs, 5 foot 4 inches woman to sue the proprietors of a public movie cinema under the Americans with Disabilities Act because she is too wide for the seats provided. Re-employment from her work in a candy factory apparently had not helped.

When "intelligence" was recently declared a socially divisive taboo term in one Southern authority recently, Psychologists were found using the term LMC to describe the cerebrally challenged, on enquiry it was established that LMC stood for low marble count. The same authority took to scrambling the ABCD labels of streamed classes without once fooling the children "Please Sir, are we the daft class?" one cheerfully enquired without a hint of concern or stigma. "Oh no" replied the teacher taken aback "but you are very special".

Euphemism, originally kindly intentioned can lead to denial, even a clinical denial of the condition. The Manchester school denied the true nature of deafness for decades and advocated "oralist" prohibition of signs in education under their cloak of euphemistic inaccuracy. By confounding "deaf" and "partially deaf" under the rubric of "hearing impaired" then it was possible to claim general success for treatments which only work with the partially deaf. The faulty logic is:

HI = D+P
O cures P
P is HI
∴ O cures HI
D is also HI
∴ O cures D

It is, of course, the fallacy of the undistributed middle where it is assumed wrongly that some HI = all HI.

In politics, the cynical use of "weasel" words has a long sorry history. Inner cities are not wantonly destroyed for profit but "developed", parties do not lose an election but "win a moral victory": George Orwell's doublethink and Newspeak were observations not fictitious inventions. In 1993, brutal massacre was sold as "ethnic cleansing" – a euphemism more suggestive of "My Beautiful Launderette" than the foul atrocity that it is. So we are back to square one with the resurgence of the views of the twentieth century's master of euphemism on a massive scale and its greatest virtuoso of oralist presentation who in 1939 proclaimed "Patients who are considered incurable on the best available judgement after crucial evaluation of their condition can be granted a mercy-killing." (A. Hitler)

This kindly-seeming death warrant made possible the legal extermination of millions: Himmler scheduled for obligatory sterilisation, an officially estimated 160,000 congenitally deaf citizens but a large unrecorded proportion of these were murdered in "euthanasia" hospitals such as Hadamar along with the known 1600 children from schools for the deaf. The death squads who practised their evil trade on the sick, lame, elderly and handicapped, including whole schools of deaf children, later turned on religious, sexual and racial deviants with the foul pollution of European civilisation which will be with us in some form or another till the end of our history.

Disenchanted with the more thoroughgoing fundamentalist advocates of politically correct relabelling, some reaction among the recipients of the new labels was to be expected. Sydney Scroggie of Dundee was one who expressed dissent from the mealy-mouthed purveyors of the whitened sepulchre.

> "We live in an age terrified of treading on people's toes or digitial extremeties. Euphemisms flourish as never before. Badly behaved becomes "emotionally disturbed", an auld mannie is a "senior citizen" and as for the beautiful word "cripple", it has quite gone out of circulation. It is too starkly descriptive for the pusillanimity of today. I speak as a blind cripple and it amuses me that the blind have now come to be called "visually handicapped", the crippled "the physically disabled". It does not seem me any longer when I am described as one of the visually handicapped, physically disabled. To be 'favouring a leg' doesn't have the dramatic force of 'lame' – there is something not quite right about being as visually handicapped as a bat.

*Were I a tink I would glory in this name and reject the nervous euphemism
'travelling person'. Were I a spade I would take serious objection to being
called an agricultural implement"* (NUD Newsletter 1980).

When those responsible for drafting the ADA anti-discrimination legislation surveyed the
opinion of the discriminated, they offered a competition for an alternative name for "disabled"
to describe this group. No better title than "disabled" was found in fact but one remarkable
suggestion was "the euphemistically challenged". This may seem implausible but was
recorded in a government report and thus must be true – honest Native American.

Sometimes minority groups have been more extreme and resorted to the Cyrano reaction.
Cyrano de Bergerac was the best swordsman in France who tended to kill people who used
the wrong euphemism to describe his incredibly long nose. From a position of strength he
had no need to be mollified by being addressed as probiscusly challenged or responsible for
increasing the number of metabolically challenged in his immediate vicinity. So we have
African-Americans who call themselves "blacks", Hearing Impaired people who call
themselves (capital) Deaf, Gays who pointedly call themselves Queers and those political
Conservatives who accept their enemies' pejorative nickname and refer to themselves proudly
as "Tories", originally the name of a particularly wild bunch of bog-trotting Irish brigands.
The mention of nationality in the last example reminds us that most nationalities save the
universally friendly Scots and Belgians have a nasty nickname inflicted upon them by
previous enemies. These are intended to be insulting and should be avoided egs;

Mick	–	Irish	Frog	–	French
Yid	–	Jewish	Wog	–	Arabian
Wop	–	Italian	Limey	–	English
Dago	–	Spanish	Kraut	–	German
Coon	–	African	Chink	–	Chinese
Yank	–	American	Nip	–	Japanese
Gringo	–	Anglo-Saxon	Gook	–	Korean

In Sign Languages comparable forms exist and one sensible diplomatic move by the World
Federation of the Deaf was the decision to get all to use the sign preferred by each nation to
describe themselves. Thus the slanted eyes sign equivalent to "Chink" is now replaced by the
outlined Mao Tse Tung jacket sign for China. The hooked nose sign equivalent to Yid is to
be avoided in favour of the two crossed forefingers representing the Star of David and flea
flicking or potato jabbing signs for Mick are better replaced with the aesthetic sign for harp –
with the risk that the latter still evokes associations with Harp lager and Guiness rather than
the ancient Ireland of Tara's halls.

A good example of the positive and negative emotional values associated with one word
throughout its usage at different times and different places is that of the Greek word for
wheel, cycle kuklos which came to English via the Latin circulus. This has survived in the
English word circus and because early Christian worshippers often took over the holy sites
of stonehenge type stone circles, in the word church. In Scandinavia, the word kirk is
identical and in Scotland the words Church and Kirk are used interchangeably. This word
with its connotations of divine dignity suffered a reversal on transportation to the new world.
Among the immigrant masses who signed on for American citizenship were many who could
not write their own name. These were obliged to sign with a cross. Some non-Christian,
mainly Jewish, immigrants objected to the sign of the cross and were allowed to sign with
a circle. This circle became the stigma of illiteracy and to this day the Slav-Yiddish for
circle, kike , is used as an insulting nickname for Jewish illiterates analogous to the Australian
"reffo" for refugee immigrants.

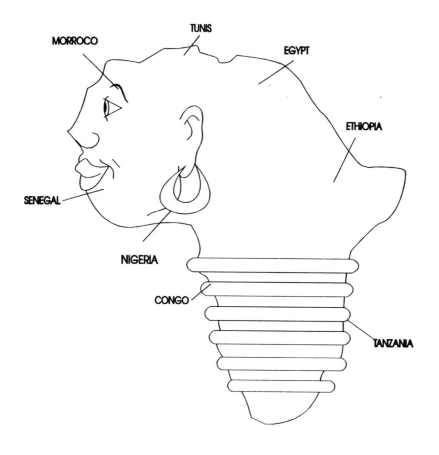

MORROCO

TUNIS

EGYPT

ETHIOPIA

SENEGAL

NIGERIA

CONGO

TANZANIA

Nationalities of Africa in Sign

The Deaf Nigerian Emmanuel Asodeh argues against politically correct signs for Africa which remove the sign from the face, making eye contact more difficult. He describes the Swahili, lingu franca, sign for Africa, represented by a "Mother Africa" beauty with a long neck upon which individual nations are set as with the Map of Africa illustrated in the drawing opposite by Colin White.

This seems theoretically tidy but conducive to misunderstanding in practice; fine for West Africa but a little difficult for Somalia and Kenya placed on the back of the head: South Africa scarcely bears thinking about.

The Chicago Sun Times (Jan 1994) noted some politically correct revisions of unacceptable stereotypes used in sign language. Some preferred the African map signs to the flattened nose or index finger across the brow to indicate black but did not explain where a Chicago African fits in on the map of Africa. Another comment was that the PC sign for Japan which replaced the slanted eye and J sign was unacceptable as it was the sign used in America for the female reproductive organ. This comment seems wildly misinformed as the Japanese sign for Japan currently used all over the world has a handshape with the thumbs below the 8 fingers, not above; a movement which draws the hands apart whilst thumbs and fingers come together, not fixed as in a citation still; is signed at neck level, not lower down and is about three times larger and like most Japanese signs elegant and aesthetic.

The Gallaudet satirical samizdat "Out of Focus" describes a recent move to eliminate politically offensive terminology from the speech, signing and writing of faculty and students. They found that most complaints of political affront came from an ethnic group previously known as WASPS (White Anglo-Saxon Protestants). "These people are upset because they see this acronym as derogatory" ... "the W at the beginning is an egregious redundancy as I've never me one who wasn't."

OK. So armed with this introduction to the complexities of the English Language, you may now decide to go ahead and write English. You will be in good company for some 700 million people all over the world use this language. At least 100 million people in China study English and the Chinese government has massive programmes of language teaching using BBC courses. In much of Europe, the Americas, India and Japan, English is the standard second national language where it is not the first. In 1991, the World Federation of the Deaf in Tokyo adopted English as its sole spoken and written language thus setting a precedent for the hearing majority in the United Nations. But international English develops a jargon of its own centring around International administration and organisation. The study of deafness, like the study of anything else, also creates its own specialist jargon. There is a special vocabulary of psychology, sociology, education and the language of science very often is totally foreign to the non-scientific reader. There is even a jargon of academic language which some think appropriate for the writing of thesis dissertations. All of this becomes a major hurdle for the deaf student or those who, for any other reason, are unfamiliar with elaborate English. The section at page 141 below lists some of the more common jargons but it is essential for students to master the special vocabulary of their subjects and the best way to do this is by writing down every new word and then expanding the vocabulary to include it – with the help of friends, tutors or interpreters if necessary.

The technicalities of academic writing are usually clearly set out in written instructions to students. These are often embedded in a mountain of forms, notices, pamphlets and booklets given to the newly matriculated undergraduate but it is essential to unearth your departmental ground rules, study them and observe them.

For example, length, format and layout of a dissertation is usually standard. For real, inspired writing the rule was laid down for the white rabbit in Alice in Wonderland (Lewis Carroll was a Don) "Start at the beginning, go on until you come to the end and then stop." There is rarely time to risk this when on a tightly timetabled academic treadmill and it is best to adhere to the ground rules on how many words per essay, per dissertation are recommended. There is usually a suggested number with a sizable plus or minus margin for individual preference. Most theses fall between the extremes of short and brilliant and long and conscientious. Whatever the final length, over-wordy and over-jargonised English does not impress. Good English is concise and whenever time permits careful proof-reading, spell-checking and editing of superfluous words helps. In writing as in whisky manufacture, condensation is a key process.

Sometimes students miss out on the aim of thesis research which is to generate and evaluate ideas. Mere collation of information does not do this. In first year essays, it is often difficult to be original in a new unfamiliar subject but it is always good practice to describe not merely what you have learned from others but what you think about their methods, their theories and the applications that they suggest.

Different tutors obviously have different ideas on essay writing and a knowledge of the expectancy of tutors, such as that detailed in admirable clarity by Chris Brand in the following chapter helps greatly. A complement to this is the expectancy of standards at various mark levels.

Essay marking is a skill which becomes more intuitive with years of experience and hence difficult to describe in any literal rule-of-thumb. However, the following example, from many others, may be a rough guide to what is required.

GRADE	"%"	CLASS	EVIDENCE OF READING	KNOWLEDGE ASSIMILATED	CRITICAL EVALUATION	PRESENTATION
A	> 75	1st	Well Read	Well Digested	Judicious	Fluent, Lively
B	65-74	2nd Upper	Knows Booklist	Digested	Evaluates	Well Presented
C	55-64	2nd Lower	Adequate Reading	Part Digested	Echoes Books	Neatly Set Out
D	50-54	3rd Bare Pass	Reading Thin	Slightly Digested	Lecture Echoes	Poor Structure
E	45-49	Borderline Fail	Little Reading	Half Chewed	Commonsense Only	Disorderly
F	35-44	Clear Fail	Little or None	Un-Chewed	Very Commonsense	Chaotic/Skimps
G	< 34	Bad Fail	None	Raw	Errors, Misjudgements	Very Skimpy

Another good source of ground rules for academic writing may be obtained from the "Suggestions to Authors" page in almost all academic journals. These give specific hints on article structure and sub-headings on layout and on referencing. It is best to begin with the good habit of correcting referencing from the earliest first year essays. All references noted should be listed in a bibliography taking the format of Name, Initials, Year, Title, Journal No. eg; Smith J (1991) Orthography in 19th Century Bulgarian. Brit J Ling.Vol 7 No 14. Publisher BPS London.

Then references may be made acknowledging material from this source simply by following quotations by (Smith 1991). This reference may be quoted by another writer or retyped using different page numbers and still be accurate. Making notes 1, 2, 3 etc or footnotes is immeasurable less efficient, necessitating a lot of tedious clerical transformations of page numbers and checking when copies are made. Careless acknowledgement and referencing could lay a writer open to the serious charge of plagiarism. Presenting others' work as one's own is a major crime as in academic life the theft of information is more serious than the theft of materials. Hence, unacknowledged looting of another person's writing usually invalidates an essay or thesis and this incurs heavy penalties.

To conclude on a more positive note, reading and writing have often been a source of life-long pleasure to many including many deaf persons. Study involves much hard work especially in the early stages for a deaf student but the rewards are obvious if we look for models in the deaf poets, authors, journalists and editors who contribute to this anthology. May they long continue to investigate, to inform, to teach, to inspire, to campaign and above all, to write for the benefit of their community and for an unknown posterity.

And if you become overly irked by the constraints of the ground rules suppressing your native, creative, talent, you can always quote Shelley at your tutor:

> *"Poetry is a sword of lightning*
> *Which consumes the scabbard that would*
> *contain it;"*

with the risk that said tutor may find statistics, accountancy and marketing more cost-effective than dead poets and awkward students.

Academic Writing: Some Advice on Essay–Writing for Undergraduate Students

by

Chris Brand – 1993

"Students probably won't read this. I wouldn't have read it. It wish I had somehow been made to read it." (A fourth–year Psychology student – who later became a Top Grade clinical psychologist....)

"Maternal deprivation lowers essay–writing ability." (Claimed in an Edinburgh Psychology 1 exam answer. – No references provided.)

(This advice was originally intended for students of psychology but may be useful for others as it has an obviously general appeal. Ed.)

The formal point of much essay–writing in universities today is to yield an assessment of your work as programmes of 'continuous assessment' require. Your essay marks or grades may be used:

a. to determine your eligibility to sit exams;

b. to modify your examination marks upwards a little when they seem unrepresentative of your work; or

c. to substitute (in whole or part) for exams in yielding your Final Course Mark. [Outright exemption from University exams may become operative only if marks from essays and practice 'class exams' reach a certain threshold level.

(Schemes of continuous assessment are popular in universities today: students are thought to like receiving 'credit' for their work through the year – and not just for a week at exam time. Continuous assessment certainly requires year–long application to meeting deadlines and accommodating 'feedback', so it is perhaps a preparation for some features of 'real life' outwith the universities.)

Educationally, the combination of essay–writing and 'tutorial group' is meant to give you a chance to practice being creative and persuasive. You might say that a tutor is a person who guarantees you an audience for your views and observations (and for your queries and academic problems) on the understanding that you'll pay sympathetic attention to the feedback. What makes a tutorial different from a mere discussion group is that you are putting forward your own work to see what response you receive from the 'expert' – and from your fellow tutees if you elect to read your essay to the group. Hopefully, tutors will remember to praise your efforts; but criticism is the quick way to improvement.

Feedback, especially negative feedback, ought to be your gain – just as it's only your best friend who'll tell you about your halitosis, so is your tutor benignly concerned with your competence and performance. Your friends, of course, won't always offer acceptable advice; but, if you want to keep them for, among other things, the times when they will, it's worth giving occasional demonstrations of your interest by manifestly transferring the advice to long–term memory. (So remember to bring a pencil to the tutorial!)

Writing Style. When you write an essay you should firmly grasp the opportunity to argue the hind leg off a donkey. An essay should no more be a dreary presentation (or even condensation) of what you've just read than would be your conversation with any other intelligent person whom you did not wish to bore. Certainly, you should present evidence for the claims and criticisms you make; and a low 'mark' will attend mere strings of generalizations and speculations. But you should always remember that, in an essay, you're trying to answer a question (or series of questions) and to argue a case for one solution rather than another. As a complement to this persuasive communication, you should remember that style is important – and, even in an essay that is to be seen rather than heard, spelling. It's not just a depressing experience for a tutor to be confronted with poor literacy; it's more that poor style spoils the image you're trying to create. Faulty literacy and bad style mean that you're seen with your hair in curlers. How much respectful attention would you pay to such a performance? The best you could hope is that tutors would be interested as parents might be in the clumsy but perhaps original productions of their children: sympathetic, but not prepared for suspension of disbelief. So don't waste your opportunity to have your 'say' by being boring or clumsy. (Resolve to accept a least a few of the suggestions from 'Tools-Grammar' on your word-processor.)

In the main body of the essay, try to avoid the use of the first and second person. It's not just a matter of appearing professional; such avoidance will normally help you to avoid irrelevance. ('We' is often tempting, but you should at least consider re-writing as 'it is a matter of common experience that...' or as 'this essay will deal with...'.) Make sure each paragraph is directed to establishing some 'point.' – you should be able to summarize that point in one sentence. Always maintain interest by using at least one example, quotation or joke in each paragraph. If, however, your writing has idiosyncratic forms of literacy due to visual anomalies or dyslexia, then allowances may be made for this and various forms of concession made to students who register with the appropriate disabled panels. (Students whose first language is not English, including some deaf students, do not by this fact alone qualify for concessions in this area.)

In **preparing for an essay**, try to:

a. make sure you know what are the two main 'sides' to the argument, and that you have some names of celebrated scholars on each 'side';

b. use the references given in course lectures, and the course textbook, so that your essay will link to your coursework and help you with eventual exam questions as well; and

c. extend the recommended reading by using the handy short articles in books like EYSENCK, ARNOLD & MEILI's **Encyclopaedia of Psychology** (Fontana), F L GREGORY's **Oxford Companion to the Mind** or U.P.G's.

The **essay** should:

a. have a 4cm left-hand margin for later notes by the tutor and by yourself;

b. have an introduction showing the importance of the topic, pointing out the main conflicts (of observation or explanation), and indicating headings to the main sections into which your essay will be divided;

c. use the headings as it proceeds – 'Is altruism personological?' etc;

d. highlight and describe at some leisure the two or three most celebrated researches, critiques or reviews on the area;

e. give references to the authority for, or detail of, claims – eg 'BLOGGS, 1984, cited by H Gleitman, 1991, Psychology, P 411';

f. have a conclusion. (**Try** to avoid 'More research is necessary'!)

Most university marking scales use a pseudo percentage 0–100 mark, with an effective range of 30–80 and a pass/fail cut off at 50. The use of mark distribution differs widely, so it is essential to make yourself familiar with the local values favoured by your own university, college, faculty and department. Here is my own summary of classical UK conventions:

49% and below	'Fail' :(Fact, tradition and conjecture are confused when actually offered.)
50–54%:	(Grade D):Class III – type work. (It is detectable that the student is reading Psychology; relevant views are mentioned.)
55–64%	(Grade C):Class II2 – type work. (Shows reasonable familiarity with main theories and perspectives without really attempting any very compelling or engaging conclusion.)
65–74%	(Grade B):Class II1 – type work. (Thorough work, clearly argued and presented; fair and well-informed; sensible and thoughtful.)
75–100%	(Grade A):Class I – type work. (Traditionally involving additionally fluency, comprehensiveness, critical ability and some originality.)

(Roughly the top 5% of University students used to be thought regularly capable of first-class work; but today 'Firsts' are awarded to 22% of students at Cambridge, 13% at Oxford, 11% at Loughborough, Salford and Heriot-Watt, 8% in Edinburgh, Manchester and London and 2% at Aberystwyth and Ulster so it is harder to see their precise, general or universal meaning.)

However, marks are only a crude guide – it's the verbal feedback that should really interest students. Short and general comments in writing may be made and a line drawn longitudinally by the side of a passage to indicate that further discussion with a tutor is suggested. The following symbols might indicate more particular comments:

Arg	=	I am wondering what exactly is your **argument** at this point.
Dsc	=	Let's **discuss** this in the tutorial – Please raise it.
Exp	=	You could helpfully **expand** on what you have said, give an example or a little evidence of your claim, or give a (complete) reference to your source.
Grm	=	**Grammar**?
Mng	=	I'm not really sure of the **meaning** at this point.
Rlv	=	I can't quite see the **relevance** of this point to our argument.
Slc	=	**Solecism**, stylistic infelicity?
Spl	=	**Spelling**?
T/F	=	I don't quite understand whether you're claiming this statement to be **true** or **false**. (Are you just quoting someone else, or merely stating a hypothesis? Or is this your own claim?)
Wrt	=	I'm afraid I can't read your **writing** at this point.

If you don't understand the point of a comment, or if you disagree, then it's up to you to ask for explanation; if you don't, the tutor will obviously make the economic assumption that nothing further is needed.

I hope this will make clear my own expectation of the form that essays should take and that it will have some general applicability. But it is also, to a degree, idiosyncratic – reflecting my own quirks. **Of course** there are other 'model' ways of writing essays. You can see them in **Scientific American, New Scientist, The Psychologist, New Statesman and Society** and **The Spectator**; and I hope you'll have a look at them. My job as your tutor at the moment is only to get you pointed **in the direction** of being able to deliver such essay work. If you're there already, I'll sit back and enjoy your prose!

Even so, my advice won't suit all of you – I can guarantee it! So please remember: this is **only** advice. Despite what I have said, I sincerely hope I would be able to recognise the sheer brilliance of the occasional illiterate, disorganized, long–winded and blatantly one–sided essay... Anyhow, the important thing is not that you should agree with all, or even most of the above suggestions, but that, if and when you should disagree with them, you will be doing so thoughtfully, in full cognizance of the options open to you. In that sense, I hope I have liberated you into **your own** idiosyncrasies. On the other hand, I'd be doing less than my duty if I gave you strong positive reinforcement for written work of a type that would not, in later life, earn the respect of the publishers, journal editors, or other professional people (doctors, judges, etc) whom you might be trying to persuade. **So, if you think there's a better way of writing essays, go ahead and persuade me! Attitude change is what the good essay is going to achieve.**

Bias & Balance in Television Writing for Deaf Viewers

by

Bob Duncan, Producer, LISTENING EYE, Tyne-Tees Television
Based on an address to the Joint Workshops With the Deaf,
Goodricke College, University of York

Chairperson, Members of these Joint Workshops.

I would like to thank you on behalf of everyone at LISTENING EYE for inviting me to speak to you today.

I was relieved when George Montgomery wrote to me in his letter:

"Please do not feel narrowly constricted by this title chosen for you – it's purely bureaucratic need to put something in the programme."

I was relieved because, although the title seems to me quite open:

"Problems of bias in TV Reporting of Controversial Areas"

George's first letter made it clearer what he had in mind when he invited me. He said:

"It would be excellent to have a .... paper from you .... on the televising of controversial areas and the need to avoid bias."

"Televising of controversial areas" – that's no problem. We do it all the time and I can talk a bit about that.

But "the need to avoid bias"? – If I took that literally, I think, as producer of LISTENING EYE, it would not ring entirely true for me to talk about "the need to avoid bias." Because LISTENING EYE has got a built-in bias, as I think even most of the viewers of our first series, which was just a wee bit 'milk-and-water' in its approach, were aware. So why, I wondered, was I being asked to talk about "the need to avoid bias."?

George explained that. In his first letter he also said:

"We get many television outfits descending on the school here, but without doubt your "Listening Eye" impressed us as the most fair and objective, i.e. unslanted, reportage that we have seen. Indeed, we have had cause to groan on occasion at the sheer amateur inaccuracy of some attempts at describing the complexity of deaf education in our locality."

Ah I see! – "Fair... objective... unslanted." That referred to a programme which we did about the education of deaf children which featured Donaldson's School in Edinburgh and a Partially Hearing Unit in Gateshead. Both used a form of Total Communication.

Fair? Objective? Unslanted? Let me read you another letter I received – just after this programme was transmitted. This came from a teacher in charge of a "Unit for Hearing-Impaired Children" at a County Junior School, "somewhere in England":

"   *Dear Sir,*

With reference to your television programme, 'Listening Eye', I would like to say how appalled I am at the contents of the series. The programme is biased and ill informed and merely serves to portray hearing impaired people as a "peculiar people", set apart and different from the rest of humanity. This need not be so. With a little more research you could at least give a more balanced view and show that deaf people can learn to talk amazingly well and take their place in society. The hearing impaired children that I teach prefer to talk than sign and make full use of their residual hearing through good hearing aids – they don't want to be seen as different and do all they can to be as 'normal' as possible. Indeed they are the same as you or I except that they have a handicap which many overcome.

Also, I would like to point our that what is signed is not the same as appears on the screen as sub-titles. Isn't this rather misleading to the general public, giving the impression that the signing is grammatically correct and signed at a normal rate of utterance? This is not the case.

I shall look forward to seeing a programme showing the success of the oral/aural approach to teaching hearing impaired children and would be happy to supply you with any material. Then your "guide to the issues facing deaf people in Britain today" would be more accurate and informed.

Yours faithfully"

Well!

"Biased... ill-informed... misleading." – "Fair... objective... unslanted." Which is right?

I would like to suggest that neither is entirely wrong.

"Fair and objective"; within our limitations and the context of the areas we've chosen to cover, we try to be. "Unslanted": – that's more problematic.

"Ill-informed"; I don't think we were in this case and I hope we're not "misleading". But "biased", as the Hearing Impaired Unit Teacher accuses; I think, by her lights – or any lights, for that matter – we certainly are. Because, although we are, I hope, w<u>ell</u> informed, we are very <u>selective</u> in the information we purvey and in the subjects that we cover. That teacher was quite right in the sense that there was a total bias in the LISTENING EYE team against featuring the kind of approach she is talking about in the way that she would have liked us to feature it.

Why?

Well, I'd like to read and third letter to you that may help to explain why – this was sent to our Continuing and Community Education Officer.

Dear Ms Brown(e)

Thank you for your letter about the programme "Listening Eye" and for the badges.

While I am sure your programme is of value to those schools who employ sign language in the education of their pupils I am sure you appreciate that it is inappropriate in those schools such as this one where a wholly oral approach is used.

As I am sure that you are aware schools differ quite radically in their approaches in order to meet the wide range of need amongst hearing impaired pupils. I suggest that you contact Gordon Mitchell, the Education Officer of the Royal National Institute for the Deaf, as he should be able to identify to you those schools which adopt a wholly oral approach and thus save you the trouble and expense of contacting such schools in the future.

Yours sincerely

What a biased person! Doesn't want our badges! Doesn't want our literature! Won't watch our programme!

What a closed mind!

So what's the situation?

We transmit our programmes into a world where everybody's biased. Everybody has preconceptions. Everybody is predisposed to believe what we say or not to believe it, to accept or not to accept, to approve or disapprove.

We live in the same world as them. We have preconceptions. How can we avoid being biased? Above all, how can we avoid being biased in our selection of material?

Our programme is twenty-six minutes long. If we give every different viewpoint equal airtime, they'll have about five seconds each and then they'll all complain about not getting a fair crack of the whip. So we've got to make choices. Some things have got to be left out. Some people have got to be left out. How do we decide? Once we've decided where to go and who to speak to, we're still selecting at every turn. We decide, after discussion, what questions we're going to ask. People may offer other comments, other contributions. Some we accept and use; some we don't. Sometimes because there isn't time for it in the programme; sometimes because we know they're wrong; sometimes because we disagree and think they're being misleading.

But we don't always reject what they say because we disagree with it. Sometimes we use what they say – although we disagree – although we know they're wrong – or, in fact, because we know they're wrong – and we want everybody to see just how wrong they are.

Terrible, isn't it?

The trouble is that, usually, half the people sitting at home watching aren't as clever as us and they don't know these people are wrong. They agree with them!

Of course, there's an element of parody in what I'm saying but you should take some of it seriously because it's impossible completely to avoid bias. Every time the director positions a camera so that the person in the frame looks bigger or smaller, more powerful or more vulnerable.....

In the case of people who use their voices, every time the sound recordist or the sound engineer tweaks the knobs to make the person's voice lighter or deeper..... Every time an interviewer is more aggressive or more engaging, speaks more loudly or more quietly or does the equivalent in sign language, asks questions that are more penetrating or that are lobbed gently in the air to be smashed back resoundingly.....

Then they – or, I should say, we – are operating within the limits of our own competence for a start (and that should never be ignored – sometimes we get things wrong because our competence fails us); and also the limits of our own ways of seeing the world, relating to people, thinking – in other words, our own bias.

Now deaf people know this.

They're quite used to people operating within the limits of their own competence – ways of seeing the world – ways of relating to deaf people – in other words, their own bias.

When I read to deaf people the letter from that headmaster – who doesn't employ sign language in the education of his pupils – who doesn't want to watch LISTENING EYE, which is presented by deaf people, in sign language..... deaf people know the score. They know people like that. They know their position. They've known it all their lives.

So what do deaf people want from LISTENING EYE? And – just so that it's clear – by deaf people I am talking about those deaf people who regard sign language as their language and who identify themselves as part of the deaf community, because they are the first, though not the only, target audience for LISTENING EYE. What do they want from us?

Do they want us to be unbiased? Well, I'm sure that on certain issues they would like us to try to be: issues internal to the deaf community, or issues that are still the subject of discussion and debate within the deaf community. On those issues I think they would expect us to try and suppress our own bias, to consult widely and to mount fair discussions, fair investigations, fair presentations, taking into account as far as we can the full range of views expressed by deaf people themselves. We will try to do that.

Unfortunately, I am a hearing person. I am the producer of LISTENING EYE. I have only a very basic working knowledge of sign language and a friendly, interested and concerned outsider's view of the workings of the deaf community. But I have got some experience of working with different communities and people and trying to make some sense of how they view their own affairs. And whatever skill, judgment, experience, I've acquired, I will try to put it at the service of the deaf people whose programme I'm privileged to work on to help them make it a good forum for discussing deaf issues, until such time as deaf people themselves have the experience to take it over. In those areas, it's a question of me, not so much suppressing my own bias, but of recognising my own ignorance – which is, perhaps, the first thing any hearing person should do! On those issues I'll try and help them strike the right balance and if particular sections of the deaf community feel that their views are being ignored or misrepresented, I hope they will complain and their complaints will be taken on board and answered or acted upon.

But when it comes to issues to do with relationships between deaf people and hearing people – the dialogue between the deaf community and the wider society – what then do deaf people want from LISTENING EYE?

Then I don't believe they do want us to be unbiased, balanced or impartial. I believe they want us to give their views priority – and I know their views may not be unanimous – but certainly to allow expression to the full range of deaf views as against the views of hearing people. That doesn't mean to exclude the views of hearing people – not even hearing people with whom most or all deaf people would disagree. Those hearing people have got to be allowed to state their arguments so that deaf people can counter them. Also, we want hearing people coming new to the issues to hear both sides and judge where the logical arguments lie. But the arguments have got to be stated and answered on ground chosen, as far as possible, by deaf people for a change.

I'd like to use an analogy; and I've got to be careful because I don't think it's an exact analogy. Recently, the BBC news, in particular, was criticised for not being impartial enough in its coverage of the issue of apartheid in South Africa. It was being too hard on the South African authorities. And a leading BBC executive replied simply, "How can you be impartial on an issue like apartheid?"

I'd like to suggest that maybe – just maybe – there are issues affecting deaf people in this country on which it is just as difficult to be impartial. Maybe there aren't any such issues, but let's consider the possibility.

If black people in South Africa were given their own television programme by the state broadcasting service, could you seriously expect them to discuss apartheid in a way that gave equal weight to both the pro-apartheid and the anti-apartheid case?

Similarly, if we were to find, in this country, that there were issues on which the majority of deaf people felt just as strongly as the majority of blacks do about apartheid, would you expect deaf people's own programme to be even-handed in its coverage of the opposing points of view? I don't think deaf people would. And if it was, I don't think they would regard it as their own programme.

So I think – in fact, I hope – that in future series you can expect LISTENING EYE to deal with certain issues in particular ways which to many people will appear biased. And, indeed, will be biased as far as possible towards the "deaf" point of view, insofar as we can establish what that is. Because there is already so much bias in society in general against deaf people's own views of their own affairs that the only way to work towards an eventual balancing out is, I believe, to allow them to express their biases for a while, until the hearing world sits up and pays attention.

Over the Wall
by
Charles Donaldson

"They called me a thief and so I became a thief" **Jean Genet**

The Deaf community arose as an unconscious celebration of a common language, Sign Language, which had for too long and by too many people been subjugated and distorted by hearing, deafened and hard-of-hearing people. It is a beautiful, subtle and expressive language, yet it is a misconception that all Deaf people have the same facility in it. As there are hearing people who are illiterate in their spoken language, there are Deaf people capable of far greater erudition in Sign than other signers.

The Deaf community also grew from the need to have a protective cocoon of identity with similar others, to share that wonderfully easy comfort of belonging in an essentially non-critical environment.

This small community slowly established guerilla outposts around the country, gaining strength from its surety in the validity of its language.

And then, gradually, hearing people became interested in the phenomenon. Like cultural anthropologists of the most arrogant type, they studied and dissected, pontificated and pronounced, giving the Deaf community a spurious academic respectability. These students of human mores defined this fascinating community according to their own values and in the worst cases sought to impose these on the Deaf community or to see them where they did not exist.

They set up university courses in Deaf studies, in British Sign Language, in Deaf culture et al, yet rarely involved the people of the tribes in their studies. They were out there, looking through intellectual telescopes, not within attempting to deepen their knowledge of what they were. They did almost as much damage as the bigoted fools of the Milan Conference.

They thought they were helping Deaf people but they were incapable of SEEING them, of joining them, most of all of belonging to them.

And they were not welcome.

For in the interim between evolving their community and receiving their new visitors, something had happened to the Deaf community. It had fossilised into a defence mechanism, stultified by the fitness of its way of life.

Its standards and patterns of behaviour were no longer a positive celebration of a shared language and heritage (often of oppression) but had become a cultural redoubt, immune to outside influences.

Anything new or different was feared and rejected. Consider, for example, this heart-rending plea for acceptance by Theona Chioccioli and friends on behalf of people like them who grew up in a signing deaf community but who are now estranged from them by an increasing loss of vision. Most of the group have Usher's Syndrome, type 1, which causes the cells in the retina of the eye to start to die resulting in a progressive blindness. Addressing the deaf community via the pages of the national deaf newspaper (Silent News, May 1994, Rochester, NY, USA) they say:

"We, as Deaf people, have always treasured our eyes, as we are sure each of you does. The visual loss started slowly, and we had to adjust bit by bit. Ultimately, the loss impacted on our lives and we had to change the way we live.

We would like you to understand us better because we have had some bad experiences with you, the Deaf community.

Some of you have no patience with us; when you see a Deaf-Blind person, you turn away, or try to avoid contact with us. Some of us have been insulted by people who thought that they were teasing us.

We have learned that many deaf people don't like to use tactual sign language; they pull away from us, which is insensitive and insulting.

Some of us have sat in our Deaf club with almost no contact from other club members and our friends for hours. We spend a lot of time alone, and when we come to the club, we are really hungry for contact, discussion, news, chatting and information. We don't want deaf people to pull away from us rejecting us because of our blindness."

"One of the difficult things about our vision loss is losing independence. We don't like to ask for help but sometimes we must ask for a ride to the store or church, or for a favor of picking up something at the store. We hate to ask. We only wish that occasionally our friends would call to see if we need anything.

We want you to ask us questions. If you aren't sure how to communicate with us, let us know. We are happy to answer questions and we will let you know if we need changes in the communication for better understanding.

We were your friends. Don't be afraid of us. Don't pity us. If you cared about us before, remember we are the same people we were.

We are each an individual with varied needs, but we find ourselves limited more and more to interacting only with other Deaf-Blind people. We want contact with Deaf people who still have vision.

We grew up with you in our Deaf world. We miss you. Please take a few minutes to be with us. Don't be afraid. We don't like being isolated."

Sadly, loss of vision was a cause of substantial rejection. Similarly, black, disabled or gay deaf people were excluded from the tribe, cast out to form their own. Deafness had become a raison d'etre, not an accepted part of one's being (or even one's whole being), but a weapon to be used in defence of the tribe's isolation.

No messengers were sent out to other cultures, no ambassadors tried to learn the language of the other (although, conversely, many of the high profile "leaders" of the deaf community had an excellent command of English!) The other had subjugated the tribe's own language, why should it now try to understand theirs?

Behaviour that had nothing to do with deafness was excused and defended as being BECAUSE of deafness. OUR prejudice is no worse than yours, so we will not abandon it.

We are a *bona fide* linguistic minority (and what DEAF person coined that expression!?) and our culture has a set of values which YOU must accede to.

And so the Deaf community ploughed its lonely furrow, content to remain in its caves of linguistic and cultural isolation, immune to the occasional blandishments of the outside world. Its members married other members, bore children to be inculcated in its values, socialised and prayed together – usually under the aegis of a hearing minister delighted with such a captive audience.

And like all societies that try to cut off the world, it is beginning to die. Modern communications means that the outside world is all-pervasive, banging on the doors to get in – even, *vide* cochlear implants imposed on the tribe's children, trying to force the Deaf community back into the fold of conformity.

The hearing world's attempts at cultural genocide having failed, forced assimilation is now the name of the game. Implants, new technology, subtitles (provided INSTEAD of Sign rather as an adjunct to it), SSE etc. are the weapons.

And now the Deaf community, that tight and introvert grouping of people with a shared language and culture, is dying. Fewer young people are joining the deaf clubs and churches but seek to integrate into society at large or form their own enclaves outside the established deaf milieu.

The tragedy is that they feel faced with an either/or choice and unable to live in both worlds – a tragedy that is mirrored throughout the world, particularly in the disintegrating countries of Eastern Europe.

If "a patriot loves his country, a nationalist hates everyone else's," then we need to work to rid the deaf and hearing communities of their nationalism.

For any society to survive and flower, it needs constant new blood bringing fresh influences and ideas. Ethnic cleansing within a community will inevitably lead to the total destruction of the whole community.

The Deaf community must embrace the variety inherent to ALL deaf people, be they black, Asian, gay, straight, young, old, born-deaf, deafened etc. and whatever their chosen means of communication. The hearing world must stop viewing Deaf people as a faulty image of themselves. Both must celebrate the wonder and beauty of the Deaf and hearing communities; both must reject the cultural insularity that poisons them both.

Perhaps then we can have a dialogue of the deaf and OUR Berlin Wall will collapse under the weight of its own contradictions.

The Vicar of Braidwood
or Why I Changed and Changed my Mind
by
George Montgomery

"And this is law
I will maintain
Unto my dying day, Sir
That whosoever King shall reign
I will be Vicar of Bray, Sir."

*The Vicar of Bray was an English clergyman of the seventeenth century noted for his
spineless facility in rapidly conforming to whatever creed was professed by his superiors.*

*The Braidwood Medal is presented annually to the prize essayist of the British Association
of Teachers of the Deaf.*

*The title Vicar of Braidwood is a purely honourary award bestowed annually by the author
of the following lines on the most duplicitous invertebrate (SIGN. TWO-FACED JELLYFISH)
of the year. The examples are freely, very freely, drawn from Scotland, Germany,
Netherlands, America and England with no apologies to monocultural isolationists, Deaf
society being highly internationalised.*

Despite the Congress of Milan
I signed my way through College
But soon converted to that plan
For stultifying knowledge.
Unto my class I'd daily list
The virtues of lipreading
And chided those who dare persist
In signing what they're needing.

CHORUS
I'll wait and wait to trim my sails
Until its safe and made good
And whatsoever wind prevails
I will be Vicar of Braidwood.

When Adolf Hitler did his best
To purify the nation
I put his theories to the test
And underwent castration.
Among my friends I oft declared
The value of eugenics
And vilified the ones who dared
To hang on to their pfennigs.
chorus

In goot Van Uden's golden tays
Ven zignink vas verboten,
Ve kept de kinter in een daze
Knot knowink vot dey wroten.
Articulatink uit deir vitz,
Mitout een zilver linink.
De kinter zittink on deir mittz
Unt neffer effer zinink.

chorus
When smart Sir Alex's shining lie
and oral methods led, Sir
A loyal auralist was I
And so they made me Head, Sir.
I scorned things deaf and, like a fool,
Condemned gesticulation.
I sought salvation for my school
In loud amplification.

chorus
When Good King Holcomb swept the land
With full communication,
A T.C. addict I became
And proselytised the nation.
I wrote and signed and speechified
Denouncing prohibition
And made a ready buck beside,
On network television.

chorus
When Warnock shook the Deaf apart
With scant consideration,
I took her message to my heart
And closed down our foundation.
I mainstreamed children to despair
In social isolation
And got an Open Uni Chair
In Pseudo–Integration.

chorus
When Noam Chomsky hit the fan
Linguistic ploys were cool, man.
I quickly learned Commancheslan
For language is a tool, man.
What Stokoe found and others claim
It strictly for the birds, man.
Interpretation is my game
– in forty–dollar words, man.

CHORUS
While Vernon fought and Jordan won
I had no time for heroes.
The only signs that turn me on
Are dollar signs with zeroes.

When Doctor House went on the loose
With profitable passion,
I eagerly confirmed his views
Put Deafness out of fashion.
Instead of all that boring rot
On care and education
We'll simply surgify the lot
With cochlear implantation.

CHORUS
I'll turn and turn
From heads to tails
To any style that paid good
And whatsoever trend prevails
I will be Vicar of Braidwood.

PUBLICATION
AND POLITICS

"A free press is a free nation"

The Intellect of Women
Graduation Address
by
Agatha Tiegel

The apparent inferiority of women's intellect is to be attributed to many restrictive circumstances. We are so accustomed to behold her in a stage of development so far below her powers that we do not apprehend the full evil of these circumstances.

The error begins before she leaves the cradle. Her sex is ever a chain and restraint. Many liberties, healthy and helpful in themselves, are denied her by the decree of a false sentiment. In childhood she is tutored in the idea that her role on the great stage of life is secondary to that of the brother who plays by her side; and all meek and docile graces are carefully cultivated in her. She is not expected to reflect for herself. As she waxes in years and height, marriage is held before her as the goal of her existence, and she sinks into a state of passive waiting. She loses her soul, in popular estimation, if she violates the conventionalities; her inherent talents are not exercised and grow rusty, as it were, for want of use; her real self lies dormant. She is content with superficiality in thought, attainments, and conduct, and forgets that she is in the world to help it by action.

Popular opinion exerts a powerful influence to hold her in this condition; a rut has been made on the highway, and the wheel slips into it easily and glides along smoothly. The centuries during which university education has been the exclusive privilege of men have done much to retard her intellectual progress, as a long yielding to one tendency makes it more pronounced. The indolence natural to all contributes its share to keeping her back. It is always more agreeable to imitate than to originate, and no woman likes to incur the often unfavourable notice which a resolute step forward on her own account is certain to draw down upon her.

But in all this there is no inferiority in intellectual capacity, but only neglect of use and tardiness of development. That such repression and restraint upon mental action are artificial has been demonstrated in all ages by women whose independence has bust every fetter and won them recognition in the fields of sciences, theology, literature, politics, and art. It is impossible to estimate the immensity of the influence that woman's mind has exerted on the history of the world, an influence silently wielded and never obtruded, but of a potency inferior to no other. If, during these ages of wrong custom, of false sentiment, she has often retained much of her greatness of intellect and soul, she will better do justice to her inborn powers when she has room and light in which to grow.

The idea is absurd that a special source of study should be selected different from the one pursued in the average college under the impression that such a selection would be better adapted to woman's needs and sphere in life. The agitation of this topic is merely the old current of prejudice against learned women turning itself into a new channel when its old one has been dammed up. No one has a right to say to a woman: "In this path of knowledge shalt thou walk, and in no other." Knowledge, like religion, admits of no trammels and no narrowing boundaries; if some peculiar form of it is not in harmony with the higher tastes and inclinations, it will be rejected.

To argue also, that a woman is not fit to be trusted with her liberty on the score of her emotional nature, her poor powers of logic and judgment, and other characteristics open to criticism, is to copy the fallacies of the opponents of emancipation, who used as arguments those very faults in slaves that slavery had produced. Woman should be free as the air to learn what she will and to devote her life to whatever vocation seems good to her. To cry out that she would be unsexed is to imply that she has not that divine element in her which is the prerogative of the highest form of creation and which craves instruction from all sources. Over and above the peculiarities which pertain to a woman as a woman are her needs as a human being. She has her own way to make in the world, and she will succeed or fail in whatever sphere she moves, according as her judgment is rendered accurate, her moral nature cultivated, her thinking faculties strengthened. It is true that we have made a start in the right direction. But that start has been made very recently, and it is still too early to pass sentence on the results. There yet remains a large fund of prejudice to overcome, of false sentiment to combat, of narrow-minded opposition to triumph over. But there is no uncertainty as to the final outcome. Civilization is too far advanced not to acknowledge the justice of woman's cause. She herself is too strongly impelled by a noble hunger for something better than she has known, too highly inspired by the vista of the glorious future, not to rise with determination and might and move on till all barriers crumble and fall.

Gallaudet
April 1893

Up for PC or Down with Sexism

by
Halla Beloff

"The Deaf...."   *"The Deaf and Dumb School...."*   Or as the 'good humoured' joke in Belfast used to go, *"The Duff and Demb School...."*

*"How are the girls managing with the typing of the **Man's Achievement** manuscript? Has the office manageress got enough manpower?"*

Do we mean what we say and say what we mean? We like to think we do. But tradition and habit may get in the way. It is worth considering the matter in some detail. And the label of "Political Correctness" should not get in the way. The heart of the language changes what PC is about is giving a more fair chance in the social world for people who have had natural justice stacked against them. Changing habits which give a negative charge to language which has been against them is the first step. Women, people with a disability, members of any kind of minority group, older women and men, members of ethnic minorities, gay women and men surely all have an interest here.

It's hard to understand why PC has aroused so much scorn and anger. What that sort of 'correctness' is about is taking the meaning of words seriously. And words aren't just formulae but do influence how we understand a subject, how we think about it and in turn how we make our own plans and behave in the area. Words are the short-hand for ideas. It is through our words and category labels that children learn what the world is about. Parcels of words and names present and represent a group of people, an issue, or a relationship. Why shouldn't we get it right?

A word should be used to mean what it says. It should as exactly as possible refer to the matter in hand. It should not contain over-tones or under-tones that bring in associations to negative and positive values which are outside the technical meaning. It is, or course, those associations which show implicit stereotypes and status traditions. They are the signals of pre-judgement-prejudice.

As languages are living, they develop, take on extra luggage on the way and sometime have to be helped to change constructively. Changes sometimes come naturally, sometimes with difficulty. Writing Christmas as Xmas is disliked by practising Christians but a lot of us don't see much harm. Calling a citizen of the Unites States who came from the Caribbean a "Nigger", today is highly offensive because the speaker is harking back to the days of slavery, discrimination and tragic oppression. Insofar as it is used by a particular speaker we can only assume that they are still in that particular time-warp, with the burden of the beliefs and attitudes of that time. Otherwise, why not use the name put forward as appropriate by the people themselves? That means calling them Afro-Caribbean people here and African Americans in the United States.

Attitudes refer to preferences but have another important point, they refer to readiness for action. It is perhaps this action potential that has worried women most. The generalised 'man' and 'he' when used in common parlance, such as, "The man we need in this job will really have his head screwed on right." will surely lead to dismay when a woman walks in for the interview... Why should she have to suffer from the handicap of having all the selection panel having suddenly and hurriedly to change their mental images?

We must all admit that our community is one of upper to lower status. Groups are not considered simply 'different'. The differences always seem slotted into a ladder with white, Anglo-Saxon, middle class men in the prime of life, (hopefully slim and with a full head of hair), somehow at the top. The groups within our community have for understandable convenience, labels and conventional language around them. The funny thing is that the labels have always been chosen by the people at the top of the pile. Now as democratic ideals give voices to more people, groups want to exercise the right to choose their own names. This is a fine way for equality to squeeze into the body politic and for the language to change in a constructive open style.

So are there any general principles? First, as has been suggested, it seems right we would follow the lead of any group involved. Should we not all be called what we ourselves find right? Second, 'people first' seems like a good concept. By that is meant that the phrase 'a person with impaired sight' or 'students with a disability' rightly gives the impression that we think of an individual or a group of people with their particular characteristic following behind, in the settings where it is appropriate to consider them. And following on from this comes the crucial point of people being different in all sorts of ways, without one characteristic flooding all the others.

The simple point is that we all hold a repertoire of roles and social identities. The writer considers herself to be a woman, middle-aged, of European origin, from a family of Jewish background, over-educated, a wife and mother of two, a social psychologist, an art-lover, voracious reader, feminist, atheist, Labour voter and so on. These are then the social categories into which she could be slotted. She would object mostly strongly to be described simply by the noun – a Jewess. This would flood her selfhood completely turning her from a multifaceted, slightly interesting kind of individual into a one-dimensional character out of Victorian novel or something... The same applies to any other person noun when it is of the lower status. One might imagine that someone described as an aristocrat might not mind so much.

Women are not 'girls' nor are they even always happy to be called 'ladies'. Ladies are, after all, well away from where the action is...

As far as women are concerned, we live in communities with a long and powerful tradition of 'superior' males holding the power – political, financial, social and personal. No wonder then that it has been found convenient to assume that maleness is the norm for human society. The term 'man' has been used to refer to everyone. We've been told that 'he' is just shorthand, it doesn't exclude women. If that's the case, why not alternate it with 'she'? The plural 'they' actually solves the problem very neatly. No more he/she bother.

By ignoring the presence of girls and women, their secondary importance is reinforced.

There are many terms like Chairman, which are now being changed. Some like Chairperson. Chair is a bit odd, but there are lots of metaphors like that. 'Head' we take for granted, the metaphorical use of Chair will soon seem ordinary. The point is to get away from the assumption that a man has to hold the job.

In day to day words, there are other labels that put women down. Why are women above the average age of puberty and indeed above eighteen and legally adults, referred to as 'girls'? Is it perhaps because that puts them in their place? "The girls in the office...." Are surely taken more seriously as 'office workers' or 'women in the office'. If just now they don't mind, they soon will.

The times are changing. Police Officer, who can be a woman or a man, is already familiar. 'Foreman' has effortlessly become supervisor, 'manpower' is 'work force' or 'human resources' and 'layman', average people. Quite easy.

In the past it was considered polite to refer to a woman as **Mrs Ian Smith**, obviously a loyal helpmeet to her spouse... Why not Fiona Smith, a person in her own right? In the same way, husbands and wives, sons and daughters, boys and girls, would work better in the cause of equality by being sometimes listed the other way round. .

This seems plain common sense to a lot of us, much more intriguing is the matter of different understanding of the same behaviour when it come from woman or men. What about ambitious men and aggressive women? The bias in our seeing and judging means that we favour achievement in men and dislike it as 'unnatural' in women. It is quite a game thinking up other examples from trusting/arrogant, persuasive/pressuring and methodical/rigid to persevering/stubborn and self-confident/arrogant. This is all parcel of the heritage of sexist attitudes that show themselves in language.

The issue is obviously highly important in the field of disability where there is a long history of people being stigmatised, pushed aside, deemed stupid, and indeed at some times thought to be ill-favoured with moral justification, if not for their bad deeds, then for those of their mother. There seems a serious argument for wiping the slate clean and from listening to the people involved to know how they would like to be thought of.

Then it indeed behoves ordinary people to fit in. If that means we have to change our vocabulary every few years, it sometimes we are asked to use two or three words where we used to use one, so be it.

People with a hearing difficulty will surely know something about prejudice and tired, old, negative attitudes. They will be keen then to get it right when thinking and writing about other groups who have not had a fair set of language labels and now want to change.

Postscriptum

While checking the spelling in this piece on my computer, I was delighted to find that it did not recognise either Nigger of Jewess as words now to be in play in the English language.

The Onset of Deaf Liberation

by

Raymond Lee

Many of you will be aware that the NUD has published a book, "Deaf Liberation", last March. But most of you will have little or no knowledge of the NUD, the book and the reasons for publishing such a book. I have quite a task here to try to satisfy your needs for knowledge and I shall endeavour to impart as much information to you as can be possible without allowing boredom to set in!

Before I can discuss the book, it is essential that you get to understand what the NUD is, and what its philosophy is. In 1976, the National Union of the Deaf was founded by a group of some 40 Deaf people and this foundation was mainly due to the then current organisations' failure, after years of existence, to shift the focus of attention from hearing people who helped to run the organisations to Deaf people who were what the organisations were for. At that time, Deaf people were nowhere to be seen or heard whilst society was applauding the work of a band of hearing people who were doing everything on behalf of the Deaf. The NUD was determined to change the situation; Deaf people must be seen and heard at all times. Deaf people must be seen to run and control their own organisations and their own destinies. Deaf people must be seen to make their own destinies. Deaf people must be seen to make their own decisions that affect their own lives and also that of those Deaf people in future generations to come. Deaf people must no longer rely on mouthpieces that are hearing people and interpreters must be used. That was the simple NUD philosophy – and basically that was it and no more.

Of course there was the question: "Can Deaf people run their own organisation themselves and survive?" The NUD decided to put its philosophy into practice. Between 1976 and 1988, NUD members made themselves be seen by the public at large – launching campaigns, demonstrations, assaults and appeals as well as giving talks and seminars amidst the heart of society at large. It made many friends and equally many enemies. The friends the NUD made were Deaf and hearing people who supported new changes and attitudes; the enemies were the oralists and a surprisingly large number of Deaf people who both adopted an apathetic attitude and resisted changes for the better. I can vividly remember Cyril Robbins and J F Hudson telling myself that the BDA had enjoyed a trouble-free life until the NUD came along and caused problems! During those twelve years, Deaf people worked for the NUD for no penny in their pockets, but just out of their love for their other unseen Deaf friends and their community. And what did the NUD achieve, or failed to achieve? The answer to that depends on how one sees it. The NUD smashed through the barriers of the BBC to make "Signs of Life" and all the TV programmes for the Deaf which you have now came from that one single programme. Was it an achievement?

In 1977, the NUD started a campaign for the acceptance and recognition of BSL – predating the US campaign for ASL by one year – and wrote articles and pamphlets on this. Today, BSL is recognised and highly respected. Was it an achievement? In 1985, the NUD offered to work with the BDA to launch campaigns and demonstrations at the International Congress on the Education of the Deaf in Manchester. The BDA rejected the NUD's offer outright and the NUD worked instead with the NWRC Branch of the BDA. And what was achieved in the Manchester campaign? Massive press and TV news coverage on a scale never before witnessed in Deaf history. Was it an achievement? Remember, the BDA which rejected NUD's offer of working jointly jumped in and in its BDA News the following month, they put the headline on the front page to read "BDA/NUD" joint venture! The NUD's last campaign was in 1988 when it demonstrated outside the Department of Education and Science in London to demand an end to integration and strict enforcement of oralism in Deaf education. Two days' worth of press and TV coverage was achieved and meetings with the Department followed. Was it an achievement? We do not know if we have achieved anything but you will tell us in good time whether the NUD has done a hell of a lot of good for the British Deaf community or not. Remember, Deaf people involved with the NUD worked for a single penny and gave up their social lives and time to do so. After 12 years of battle fatigue, the NUD took a 5-year respite. It is due to re-emerge next year – fresh and vigorous, ready for the next campaign ahead.

One of the saddest things about the British Deaf community is, until as recently as 5 years ago, its lack of recorded history and this situation is, thank God, being remedied. A lot of work is being put into effect to piece together the Deaf's history. Peter Jackson made an excellent attempt with his "Britain's Deaf Heritage". One must make no mistake that this work is a truly great advance in spite of some inaccuracies, and with a leaning towards the BDA environment. Jackson's work covers only a small corner of the whole cube that is British Deaf History. There is more to dig up and unearth – and so much to do. The NUD is a strong believer in recording works and events for historical preservation. With this in mind, the NUD persuaded Arthur Dimmock to write "Cruel Legacy" and saw it published by SWP in 1993. "Deaf Liberation" is another book in which the NUD recorded and preserved Deaf people's papers given during the years 1976–86. And I would like to talk to you about it.

The inspiration to publish Deaf Liberation came to me during an heated argument with a group of oralists at the International Congress on the Education of the Deaf in Manchester, 1985. One afternoon after Dr Dale gave his paper on Individualised Integration and avoided being questioned, there were protests from a Deaf group that Dr Dale was being evasive in facing a barrage of questions which would certainly have exposed his paper and philosophy as flawed and littered with hogwash. Later after the meeting I was approached by some of Dr Dale's supporters, the Daleks (Exterminate! Exterminate!), and they started to argue that I was being a bloody minded enfant terrible, who was only out to seek trouble and who was, to put it in a nutshell, not "intelligent enough to see the wisdom of Dale's works and efforts to help Deaf children". The Daleks mentioned all the wonderful books and papers written on Deaf education and quoted Dale, Van Uden, Thomas Arnold, Sussanah Hull, Arthur Kinsey, Dr David Buxton and a few more which escaped my memory. The Daleks seemed to remember all the works of oralists past and present. I was then challenged to produce or give details of one book, written by the Deaf, to support deaf people's case for their preferred method of communication and education.

A year was to pass before I became a reader in the British Library to discover what books were available to unearth snippets of names and events to piece together a picture of Deaf history. I came across a book, "Speech for the Deaf", which was a collection of essays written for the Milan International Congress, 1880. And what did I find? Along with a full account of the proceedings of the infamous meeting, I found a collection of papers by – Sussanah Hull, Dr David Buxton, Arthur Kinsey, Mr & Mrs B St John Ackers and E Symes Thompson. One book. Same names as those quoted by the Daleks the year before in Manchester. Papers published in September 1880. Still remembered and quoted in August 1985. I started to become aware of the power of the published word. And also the power of written English.

Books can last for centuries. Books are constantly consulted for both research and reference. Books are a source of inspiration and influence. Books are powerful. And so is the Word. The oralists have written, and still are writing, books on their methods and beliefs, ensuring that the authorities are not without a copy. To counter this, what can the British Deaf offer?

The answer is almost threadbare – with the exception of Scottish Workshop Publications which was the first to encourage, take up and publish works by Deaf people, notably those of Hay, Holmes, Ladd, Lawson, Dimmock and King Jordan. I am also a proud owner of two SWD classics; "Of Sound and Mind" and "Integration and Disintegration of the Deaf in Society". The NUD decided to publish its collection of papers by Deaf people with one aim in mind – that sometime in the near future a new generation of people, educators or philosophers, disillusioned with the current affairs of Deaf education under oralism, may come across the book and be inspired by what they read. The book was not published for the glory and the immortality of the authors so that their names shall live on. Far from it, the book is there as a genuine cry for help for the British Deaf community, not least of all for the 54,000 Deaf children currently languishing in mainstreamed environment in hearing schools – both Partially Hearing Units and in individualised integration surroundings.

Another reason for publishing Deaf Liberation is the NUD wanted the book to be used as a guide for new and future generations of Deaf people who may want to form pressure groups. Deaf Liberation consists of 30 papers, of which only three were written by hearing persons – Harlan Lane contributed two papers and Dr Reuben Conrad wrote "Towards a Definition of an Oral Success". Twenty-seven papers were written by Deaf people themselves. The papers include Ladd's classic "Epistle of the Teacher of the Deaf" series, Woolley's two marvellous papers on TV and the Deaf and a good number of papers from Dimmock which are varied and diverse, covering issues from education to employment and human rights to thought process. When I first started work on Deaf Liberation, I was confronted with some 48 papers and I had to whittle down the papers to around 30 to fit into the book. And before I go any further, I would like to impart to yourselves some of my experiences whilst working on Deaf Liberation.

The first thing any person wishing to create a book needs is good planning at the outset. What purpose do you want the book to serve? What kind of readership is the book aimed for? What kind of theme should the book contain? And in the case of Deaf Liberation, should English be rigorously edited to make it easier for Deaf people to read? These were the questions I was faced with. As an editor, very often the final decisions lie with myself. I was fortunate enough to have excellent co-operation from members of the NUD Steering Committee throughout every stage of the book from inception to conception.

The purpose was simple enough – to make a lasting reminder to society of what the Deaf have been telling them in the past. The book itself was intended to be there to counter any works of the oralists in print. Having established a purpose, I then had to choose a theme in order to create some sensibility and consistency within the book. As NUD papers were varied, it was becoming slightly difficult at one stage to put them all together under one binding. This was overcome during a Sunday afternoon drinking session when an idea hit upon myself that the theme should be "Deaf Liberation" – that year in 1976 when a group of Deaf people broke away from traditional silence and liberated themselves by speaking out. It must be pointed out here that the actual words "Deaf Liberation" were first uttered by Maggie Woolley at one meeting to discuss the book. On top of that, 1976 was also considered a historical point in time when the NUD came into being. So the shape of the book began to emerge and the end product became like this: the book is a history of Deaf people's struggle and fight for their rights and needs as seen through a series of papers. And that was it – so it seemed. But then there was the question of which papers should be included and which should not be included. This was a difficult decision but in consultation with the Steering Committee a final list of papers were agreed and 33 papers were chosen.

After much work in laying out the contents of the book, shuffling around papers, shuffling them around again and finalising the product, Deaf Liberation did not look in any way good.

A book with a straightforward series of papers looked rather flat and devoid of feelings. To counter this, I added a series of prefaces preceding each paper, or a group of papers and the book looked much better. But from the historical aspect, there was something not quite right. It was at that stage when work on Deaf Liberation was severely delayed for up to 6 months ..... until I discovered that the solution to the problem was to bring in outside papers to bolster the 'sagging' weakness. It dawned on myself that NUD's history is incomplete without SWD's "Bulgaria Paper" as it inspired the NUD to write the "Charter of Rights of the Deaf". Also Harlan Lane's "Why the Deaf are Angry" given at NUD Convention in Manchester 1985. Those three papers played a vital part in NUD's history and were then included in the book and the historical aspect of the book started to take shape. However, there was still something wrong. Something not quite right. Something missing. The book was read over and over again and again. There was still a void ..... until Ladd wrote to ask if I had included Conrad's paper given at Harrogate RNID conference in 1976. That was it! I ended up with 37 papers and it became too expensive to publish. Sadly I had to get rid of 7 papers to reduce it to 30. And now, the final problem; what kind of readership and what about the English being too difficult for Deaf people at the most.

The NUD decided the book should be aimed for general readership, meaning in the main the hearing population. English, therefore, was not made any simpler for Deaf readers. Altering and severely editing papers for the sake of making them simple to read and be understood by Deaf people, whose English leaves a lot to be desired, would have completely destroyed the meaning, the power, the sense and the heart of each paper in the book. We did not want the papers to become meaningless kindergarten version of what they really are – so the matter rested there.

What I am trying to say here are two things. One, with some thought and a little help from one's friends, it is not impossible for a Deaf person to write and/or create a book of his own choice. If Deaf Liberation is anything to go by. It is an example to show that Deaf people can do it. Deaf people can write and publish – if they can grasp and master the fundamentals of English. And two, along with Arthur Dimmock's "Tommy" and Peter Jackson's "Britain's Deaf Heritage" as well as "Deaf Liberation", books published by Deaf people should inspire other Deaf persons to seriously consider looking to that path of writing and publishing. It is a present day tragedy that a lot of Deaf people have great difficulty in that field. There are many great Deaf BSL orators and they could "write" in video. But videos are more restricted than books; they cannot be read on a nice sunny day in the park or by the seaside. This raises an educational issue of great importance ..... how best to acquire English proficiency through the use of sign language. This is an important issue which cannot be ignored. It seems that BSL is not a good medium through which to learn English. It is important that Total Communication should be seriously used in all schools for the Deaf. This issue would require to be vigorously discussed among yourselves in the not too distant future. The NUD stated in its "Rights of the Deaf Child" some twelve years ago the importance of Total Communication in the education of Deaf children and this position has not changed.

Deaf people in the NUD were fortunate enough to be able to read and write English in spite of the horrendous education system they suffered. We all shall cherish the day when a good number of Deaf people start to write and publish books. We hope that that day will not be far off. As for the part of the authors of papers in Deaf Liberation, they would have never written such papers without information and personal experiences from members of the British Deaf community. What they said were noted and included in the papers. So that book, "Deaf Liberation", is theirs indeed; not the authors'. And when I am saying to all of you Deaf people that is your book, I am saying it with the blessing of every author in the book; we all genuinely mean it from the bottom of our hearts.

The Deaf Samizdat

by

George Montgomery

*"For as long as there are two
deaf people upon the face of
the earth and they get together,
so long will sign remain"*

The Cleveland Leader
December 1910

Apart from the generously subsidised journals of the Deaf Establishment like, Talk, Hark, Hearing, Focus, The American Annals of the Deaf and British Deaf News, there has always existed an important few of those minority news–sheets broadcasting advanced and usually dissident viewpoints. The Russians call such a newsletter samizdat and the word has now become a lexical import acceptable in English which has no special word for the concept. The respect for the samizdat gained ground during the existence of the former USSR when many samizdat editors could be found securely housed in government subsidised residences in Siberia.

The first deaf samizdat, expressing the grass roots viewpoint of those within the Deaf community made a late appearance in history as it had to wait for the appearance of general literacy among Deaf people which in turn had to wait upon a systematic educational regimen for Deaf children. The pioneers of Deaf education tended to be the privileged offspring of royalty, aristocracy and the well–to–do. These pupils by inclination and rank found little in common with ordinary Deaf people and they fitted in to the establishment of their day with little or no thought of changing it. Not until the time of Abbé de Le Epée and Sicard did literacy spread to Deaf children lower down on the social scale.

By 1830 Deaf people in France found the yoke of hearing guardians increasingly oppressive and Ferdinand Berthier, Claud Forestier and Alphonse Lenoir, three well–educated students of the great deaf teacher Jean Massieu, founded a deaf backlash group. From the outset, it was evident that their command of the French language was a powerful resource with which to influence general public opinion. In time their movement attracted Roche Ambriose Auguste Bébian, the highly literate son of an expatriate aristocrat, author of influential books on language and education and auxiliary teacher in Abbé Le Epée's school at St Jacques. Bébian, a hearing man fully immersed in the Deaf culture and Sign Language, was victimised by oralist educators and dismissed from his post. This perceived injustice embittered Bébian who fuelled the deaf resistance movement with high octane literary energy writing, printing and publishing a flood of papers on language, education and communication in newspapers, periodicals, magazines, samizdat and anything which would counter the dead hand of oralist conformity.

The power of the written word is in its persistence and durability over a wide area and over a long time. Thus it was not surprising that even the King of France became aware of the Deaf viewpoint by way of Bébian's prolific output. But what was surprising was that King Louis Philippe actually did something about it and invited Berthier and Lenoir to dine with him, a meeting which was said to result in the reform of education of the deaf and in the establishment of the Societé Centrale for the aid and education of deaf–mutes. As Arthur Dimmock observed in his "Cruel Legacy" (1993) this society was a pioneer in respecting the validity of the deaf "consumer" view of education. Prior to this, to borrow a Scottish Deaf comment "They asked everyone about the standard of cooking except the person who ate the meal" (SWD 1980).

Central to the schism between deaf views and other educators was the attitude to the use of signs in education. Berthier and his allies were fluent in written French and manual French (signes methodique) as well as in French Sign Language (signes naturelle). This gave them a sound communication base for their literary educational and then political activities. An early, very popular, form of "sign workshop" was that very French vehicle of culture, the banquet. Beginning in 1834, Berthier and his group organised annual banquets in Paris. Many talented Deaf people attended these banquets and the high level of culture and civilisation was an impressive exercise in public relations for the Deaf community. In particular, the eloquence and intelligence of the speeches was remarked and recorded many times by appreciative and often astonished hearing visitors, many of them eminent in their own right.

The minutes and records of banquet speeches laid the foundations of Deaf writings. Berthier was able to contribute items in the comprehensive "Code Napoléon" which accepted the legal rights of Deaf citizens to use their own "Signes Naturelle" in 1868. Not until the combined European Community ruling of 1990's has this legal recognition of their native sign languages been accorded to the other countries of Europe.

It is important to note, as the great Edmund Burke emphasised, the difference between vague lists of "rights" which are a mixture of hopes, claims and wishful thinking and properly legislated legal rights. The deaf rights of the Code Napoléon like the American Bill of Rights are soundly backed by the full legal authority of the state and defensible in the national courts. Without legal status, lists of "Human Rights", "Rights of Man", "Right to Equal Opportunities" can easily become vacuous slogans.

Nevertheless, from the listing of "rights" – a popular activity of English revolutionaries and their French and American imitators – a more general literature of protests and assertion of minority views rapidly developed. In the last quarter of the nineteenth century, the French Deaf community produced at least 15 Samizdat journals written by deaf people whose high literary standards were a credit to their educational system before it was destroyed by the infamous Milan decision to ban Sign Language use after 1880.

The French example was restricted in impact in Britain, due to the military rivalry of the two nations but it was usually welcome in America and in Scotland which has always valued the "auld alliance" with France. Thus the first British samizdat of the Deaf was "The Edinburgh Messenger" in 1843. In 1847 the "American Annals of the Deaf" appeared and still flourishes today as the oldest educational journal in the Western hemisphere under the judicious, responsible eye of editors of the calibre of Powrie Doctor, McCay Vernon and Don Moores who ensure it is no fossil.

The teaching of printing in schools for the deaf ensured a strong representation of deaf workers in the printing trades. School children often exercised their skill in school magazines such as "The Californian Palms", "The Donaldsonian", the "Kentucky Standard" and "The Communicator" of Indiana School. The role of the British Columbian "B.C. Deaf Advocate" magazine in the 1978 successful publicity campaign to keep Jericho Hill School open in the face of ill-conceived plans to close it in favour of mainstream provision at the height of the integration crusade is a classical gem of deaf history showing how the Deaf community must constantly act together to prevent inappropriate legislation by those ignorant of the particular needs and conditions of deafness. This was not the first time that an amateur magazine showed the full power of the press in challenging this kind of injustice.

In 1887 "The Silent Worker" was first printed at the New Jersey School for the Deaf and was an early advocate of what later became known as Deaf identity and the Deaf community. The response of deaf students and adults was positive and widespread far beyond the boundaries of the school gateway. Editor, J H McFarlane shows the nationwide influence of deaf jounalists in an article called "Deaf Editors of the Little Paper Family" which appeared in the Silent Worker of December 1914. He desribes the Staunton Convention of deaf editors which met under the auspices of the American Organisation of Instructors of the Deaf in June 1914. A photograph showing over 30 deaf editors records that the banquet method of exchanging ideas was still popular.

McFarlane mentions many individuals of the "Little Paper Family" (how he would have leapt on the word 'samizdat') some of which still survive. He lists among others:

The Frat, founded in 1909, edited by F P Gibson which circulated 2000 copies monthly from its Chicago base.

The Kentucky Standard, edited 30 years by "Col" McClure, a patriarch from the Isle of Skye, Scotland.

The Iowa Hawkeye whose 3 man editorial board included that celebrated ace of fingerspellers, Howard Hofsteater.

The Deaf Carolinian edited by Ms Olivia Grimes, a pioneer of female deaf journalism and the only woman editor at the banquet.

The Daily Nonpareil	The North Dakota Banner
The Nebraska Journal	The Southern Optimist
The Louisiana Pelican	The Buff and the Blue
The Silent Hoosier	The Virginia Guide
Florida School Herald	The Palmetto Leaf
The Deaf-Mutes Journal	The Minesota Companion
The Chautanqua Star	The Cleveland Leader

Naturally, deaf writers and editors were wholehearted supporters of sign language in the combined method of education and this became regarded askance by the mainly hearing educators of the 1920's who wished to impose an oralist ban on signing in school. The schism became total after a crisis when the school superintendent, Alvin Pope, issued a papal edict dismissing a number of deaf teachers for the heresy of manualism, eventually forcing the resignation of the editor George Porter in 1929.

Deaf resilience under intimidation is not so easily defeated and "The Silent Worker" was later taken under the wing of the National Association of the Deaf and soon became the official house-journal of that association, one of the biggest Deaf organisations on earth. In 1964 it changed its name to "The Deaf American" and thrives today as a major national and international forum of deaf culture and deaf opinion. The open, democratic and liberal ethic which ensured its victory over those who would censor, restrict and suppress ideas, is reflected in the editorial policy discussed in the contribution in this volume by Mervin Garretson, current editor of Deaf American monographs (Gannon in Van Cleve 1987).

When that inspired Irish alumni of Gallaudet, Francis Maginn, founded the British Deaf & Dumb Association in 1890, his revolutionary proposals were backed up to the hilt by the deaf editor of the monthly "Deaf and Dumb Times", Charles Gorham. The January issue of that year publicised the need for a national forum for the British (then including all Ireland) Deaf community and printed an appeal from Maginn to establish what is now the largest Deaf organisation in Europe, the BDA.

Maginn had many far-sighted ideas, ahead of his time and consequently died a disappointed man when his ideal of a Deaf leadership was compromised. This accounts for much of the apathetic reaction of most deaf people to their nascent national association. Ernest Abraham, editor of the monthly "British Deaf Mute", in true Samizdat style, dismissed the ruling clique of BDDA officers as inefficient and responsible for the conformist, narrow unpopularity of the association among the very people who might be expected to give wholehearted support.

Not until over one hundred years later did Maginn's ideal bear fruit but his spirit must now truly rest in peace with the appointment in 1995 of a fellow Irishman Jeff McWhinney as the first deaf chief executive. Meantime, from 1906 to 1935, some deaf autonomy was regained in the Association when William McDougall, a former pupil and later pupil-teacher of Donaldson's Hospital (now Donaldson's College) in Edinburgh, became Honorary Secretary from 1906 until 1935. The Deaf Quarterly News recorded memorably his complete identification with the association: "The BDDA is Mr McDougall".

Another Donaldsonian, Ernest Aycliffe, became president of the BDDN from 1920 to 1947. As founder-editor of the Deaf Quarterly News, Aycliffe saw it develop from a newsletter Samizdat in 1905 to an influential quarterly contributing greatly to assuage the great need for experienced realistic information about deafness in the climate of his time in Europe. (Grant 1990).

In the 70's when the work of William Stokoe on the linguistic validity of sign languages began to have an impact on the prohibitionist educational establishment in America and Europe deaf people began to take new encouragement and sought afresh to gain recognition for their views.

The total communication movement initiated by a deaf teacher Roy Holcomb codified much of the resistance to the educational ban on signing and it was publicised widely through a vividly alive series of samizdat which combined great wisdom and shrewd experience with the occasional zap of near-scurrilous satire and downright ridicule. For example, the Indiana Communicator constantly countered ignorance of deaf culture with factual missives such as "More than 40 schools for the deaf were founded by a deaf man but there is none in which a deaf man is head today" (1967). "Show and Tell" printed in Deerfield, Illinois, USA in the 70's was another Samizdat which did not pull its punches, comparing parents who allowed their children to be taught by non-communicating teachers to those who would allow their children to undergo surgery by a butcher rather than a qualified surgeon. Those handicapped people who conformed slavishly to the orthodox oralist hegemony of the time were contemptuously referred to as "Phuts", an evocative label suggesting the last gasp of something or other but derived from the initials of "Physically Handicapped Uncle Tom".

In Scotland the Scottish Workshop with the Deaf launched a similar pro Total Communication campaign through the medium of conferences and the publication of conference papers rather than by the samizdat. In England, however, the National Union of The Deaf made its "NUD Newsletter" a major instrument of change. Eventually, most of the cream of NUD Newsletters was churned into a more solid book on "Deaf Liberation" which is described in the article by Raymond Lee in this volume. One of the most intellectual and least cautious of world deaf organisations, NUD loses a little of the impact of the original letters when on its best behaviour in Deaf Liberation. Among its highlights were the genocide charges submitted to the United Nations, steadfast opposition to the destruction of deaf culture by closing schools for the Deaf, pioneer consumer-led television features on Deafness and the exposure of the 'bionic miracle' merchants portraying cochlea implants as a cure for deafness. We also treasure a few gems from the lunatic fringe in their uninhibited correspondence columns, even including the letter which accused hearing people of causing all deafness due to the effects of the second world war which they also caused.

In France the spirit of Berthier never died but surged ahead in new garb in the prolific output of Coup d'Oeil a mimeographed samizdat cum journal containing digests of researches in sociology and linguistics along the lines of Stokoe's "Sign Language Studies" with more polemic papers urging the use of sign in child development and education. The high level of discussion in Coup d'Oeil does credit to the intellectual standard of the French Deaf tradition and to the clear vision and foresight of fondateurs Bernard Mottez and Harry Markovicz.

It is a measure of the success of information campaigns on behalf of the Deaf community that, to some extent, Samizdat publications are themselves victims of this success, as their advanced ideas slowly become accepted and digested by the established majority. For example, the Deaf President Now campaign which established King Jordan as Gallaudet's first Deaf President was irresistible in its power and force. It received widespread support from established institutions and journals unlike their die-hard opposition to the Total Communication campaign. Thus the DPN campaign did not need to rely so heavily on the samizdat and fringe opinion.

In the course of time it is not unknown for an avant garde samizdat to become established and respectable. For example, the pioneer "Deaf Broadcasting Campaign News" gained the support of RNID and BBC to develop into the respectable "See Hear" magazine and we have already noted how "The Silent Worker" evolved into "The Deaf American".

Deaf concerns have a priority over social and political traditions which is a source of great positive cohesion for divided humanity. In 1991 the World Federation of the Deaf adopted one visual and one auditory world language for international communication – a move ahead of its United Nations parent organisation. At the height of the cold war American and Russian deaf educators found themselves in close agreement over the oral-manual issue. Similarly at the peak of the troubles in Northern Ireland Deaf delegates at conferences crossed sectarian boundaries with ease. The pages of "Stille Boodskapper" over the past 20 years in South Africa, whilst far from radical, reflect a total respect and harmony of deaf people from the different racial communities which is a model for the bitter racially divided hearing communities in that beloved country.

At present fax sheets, packet radio and e-mail supplement the postal dissemination of the written word. Already deaf conferences of participants spread over a wide geographical area have been conducted via the telephone e-mail link to personal computers. If a free press is a free nation then a free keyboard is no less a crucial keystone of our general liberties. The electronic samizdat is already with us and we close with a salute to all those not so mute nor inglorious Miltons resting their keyboard-hammered fingers on the way to corporate literary immortality.

Stille Boodskapper
(in English and Africaans)
Private Bag X04
Westhoven 2142
South Africa

Coup d'Oeil (French)
c/o Ecole des Hautes Etudes
en Sciences Sociales
54 Boulevard Raspail
75270 Paris Cedex 06
France

NUD Newsletter
288 Bedfont Lane
Feltham
Middlesex
London TW14 9NU
UK

Deafness/British Deaf News
BDA
38 Victoria Place
Carlisle CA1 1HU
UK

See Hear
105 Gower Street
London WC1 AH
UK

Breakthrough
(Newsletters & Reviews)
Birmingham Centre
Selly Oak Cottages
Bristol Road
Birmingham B29 6LE
UK

"The Communicator"
Indiana School for the Deaf
1200 E 42nd Street
Indianapolis
Indiana 46205
USA

"The Californian Palms"
California School for the Deaf
Riverside
3044 Horace Street
California 92506
USA

Talk
45 Hereford Road
London W2 5AH
UK

Gallaudet Today
800 Florida Avenue NE
Washington DC 20002-3695
USA

Signs for our Times
Linguistics Research Laboratory
Gallaudet College
Washington DC 20002

BC Deaf Advocate
2076 E 3rd Avenue
Vancouver BC V5N 1H7

Focus
    Division of Public Affairs
NTID, RIT
52 Lomb Memorial Drive
Rochester NY 14623-5604
USA

American Annals of the Deaf
5034 Wisconsin Avenue NW
Washington DC 20016
USA

Show and Tell
1400 Sanders Road
Deerfield
Illinois 60013
USA

WFD News
(Voice of Silence)
PO Box 65
    SF-00401 Helsinki
FINLAND

Link
NAD
25 Lower Leeson Street
Dublin 2
EIRE

Silent News Inc
1425 Jefferson Road
Rochester
New York 14623 3139
USA

Communicating Specialist Knowledge
by
Dr Elizabeth R Mapstone

We are all in some sense specialists. We all spend our days preoccupied with concerns that some other people share and many others do not. Just as people without hearing have a very specialised knowledge of deafness compared to those with hearing, so mothers have more detailed knowledge of caring for babies than non-mothers, teachers have more specialist knowledge of teaching than non-teachers, shop-keepers have more specialist knowledge of retailing than those not in the trade. You may think this is perfectly obvious. However, I have found that the consequences of this specialist knowledge are not so obvious. People who share knowledge can communicate in a deeper and more satisfying way because they share assumptions, they develop a specialist language that carries meanings no outsider can pick up. Though many academic disciplines and highly paid professions develop specialist jargon, designed to signal membership of their specialist groups and to exclude outsiders, jargon is not essential. We all can confuse and baffle others who do not share our special knowledge.

This chapter was originally written for psychologists, but it illustrates quite well, I think, how widespread is the need to think about communication. To non-psychologists, no doubt, all psychologists should be able to communicate with each other, even if they do tend to baffle anyone else. The fact is, however, that psychologists (like other academics and professionals) have to specialise, and they find it extremely difficult to communicate with other psychologists outside their particular field. This is especially the case when they come to write. All psychologists learn to write what is known as "academic style", using concepts and terminology comprehensible only to the special few in their specialist field.

I was asked to develop a new magazine for members of the British Psychological Society which would enable psychologists to communicate with each other, and with the outside world. **The Psychologist**, born January 1988, was the result. As you will see, not everyone was happy at first with the idea. Not everyone understood that communication is difficult, and that writing for the non-specialist is a craft they needed to learn. The original version of this chapter was published in **The Psychologist** of December 1993, under the title "How to write for The Psychologist". I hope the principles it outlines will be helpful for anyone who wants to communicate specialised knowledge to those who do not have it.

The Beginnings

In the early days of **The Psychologist**, our concern about the craft of writing was not widely shared. Indeed, there were those who mocked and derided our efforts to make features lively and accessible to a wide audience. "No, thank you, I shall publish in a proper journal," said one distinguished academic when invited to contribute. "Can't be doing with that," said another. "It's more like *The Sun*."

I am glad to report that both these critics (who shall remain nameless) have since seen the light, and in proper Damascene manner are converts actively working for our cause. For our aim is simple and thoroughly respectable: it is communication.

Communication requires good writing. You, the writer, wish to convey to some other person, the reader, some information you suppose that other person should have but does not. The reader may think s/he does have the information, thank you, or may not wish to know anything about it anyway, or may totally disagree with your approach, or just find it boring.

Whatever the topic you wish to communicate – a set of facts, a theory, a discovery, an idea, a joke, a bit of gossip – you have not succeeded until the reader has read and understood what you have written.

You may think this is self-evident, and about as helpful as the BBC weather man forecasting hurricanes. But consider further. We all tend to spend most of our time talking to and writing for people who share our assumptions. Cognitive psychologists communicate with other cognitive psychologists; clinical psychologists communicate with clients seeking their help or with other clinical psychologists; occupational psychologists communicate with their clients in management or with other occupational psychologists. All specialists develop their own language, theories and concepts which resonate with multiple meanings for members of the specialist group. But what happens when the specialist wishes to communicate with people outside that special group? Those concepts and theories deployed so effortlessly at work are very often incomprehensible to the outsider, and must be translated into a language the non-specialist can understand.

Even worse, the specialist may use everyday words, which the outsider understands in a different way. Just to take a simple example, consider "social facilitation": to a non-psychologist this means "making communication easier among people in a social situation"; to a social psychologist, it means "performance of a task improves when others are doing the same thing". Remember Jerome Bruner's words: in all our interpretations of what people do and say, we go "beyond the information given" and use our own knowledge, experience and assumptions. The deaf reader will readily understand this difference as the word "deaf" means very different things to those with and those without hearing.

Until very recently, almost all discussions involving deaf people ended up discussing communication, whatever the original topic chosen. "Communication" is now a buzz word for hearing people as well, and the recent government White Paper on Science proposes that all scientists embarking on a PhD should receive "communication skills training". But for the past six years, we on the editorial staff of **The Psychologist** have been emphasising that contributors need to write in a lively and accessible way if they are to communicate their ideas to others outside their particular field.

This chapter, written as I prepare to move on to pastures new, is designed to explain just what is meant by accessible writing, and I will do this by comparing and contrasting writing for a wide audience with standard academic journal style.

Audience is the Key

The Psychologist aims to "communicate the same kind of information normally found in academic journals to psychologists with a wide range of academic and professional interests" (see Information for Contributors). This clearly implies that you could not differentiate academic and feature writing simply on the basis of topic.

The essential difference between an academic paper and a feature is in its presentation: this includes such things as title, opening paragraphs, structure of article, prose style, language. Presentation of any topic depends upon the audience intended to read the paper.

Writers hoping to be published should ask themselves this important question: Who will want to read this paper?

The answer should not be just your colleagues and peers: you have probably got a number of specialist journals waiting for such material. The answer should be one of a number of variations on the theme "anyone interested in psychology pure or applied", whether academic or student, professional or amateur. Academic contributors in particular should remember that they are a minority of the membership (approximately 10 per cent), even though what they have to tell us may well be of primary importance.

The potential audience for writers in **The Psychologist** is nearly 20,000 psychologists, in a wide variety of occupations, aged from late teens to extreme old age, and so with enormously varied experience and knowledge; journalists and broadcasters, national and local; government officials, politicians; interested outsiders who pick it up in libraries.

First Catch your Reader

Very few people ever sit down and read professional magazines from cover to cover, so you have to capture your reader. Title should be short and snappy, witty if possible, certainly inviting. The introduction – those sentences in large bold type which take the place of the academic abstract ("standfirst" in publisher's jargon) – should explain why the reader will find it worthwhile to read on. Most people will decide on the basis of the title and introduction whether to stop and sample, so both must be clear, jargon-free and must never mislead.

This is where an editor can help. The editor should be prepared to invent the title and write the introductions, with your approval. Pictures, too, invite the browser to pause, and the editor will seek out suitable illustrations if you cannot suggest them. From this point, though, it is up to you.

Your opening paragraph should state your theme. The reader has paused in a riffle through the pages with the thought, "This might be interesting" – convince her/him to stay with you. Right from the start there should be no doubt where you are going, so begin by stating clearly, in terms which may be understood by a non-specialist, what you are about to discuss, and where it will lead.

This is quite different from an academic article, where the standard Introduction gives background, and frequently the reader is left in suspense about a final outcome until the standard Discussion and Conclusions. Even abstracts may promote a mystery by simply promising discussion of issues. This may be good academic writing, but feature writing is more like quality journalism: the reader needs to know that it is worth spending time on your paper.

Language

An academic paper clearly signals that its audience is intended to be those for whom academic presentation of information, evidence and discussion of issues is the clearest and most appropriate medium. Such an audience may be assumed to have specialist knowledge, and to share key concepts, theoretical constructs and knowledge of the literature. These assumptions lead to the use of specialised language, or jargon which conveys information swiftly and efficiently to those who share the knowledge, but which baffles and alienates those who do not.

Of course an academic journal article may occasionally be read by non-academics. Sometimes they are written so clearly and are so intrinsically interesting that they are accessible to a wider audience, even when their **structure** is essentially that of an academic article. However, on the whole, non-academics do find the standard academic article difficult of access.

A key difference between academic and feature writing lies in choice of language and voice. Good feature writing requires concrete detail and the active voice, while academic papers tend to use abstract concepts and the passive voice.

A concrete example will help. Take the sentence, "The employability of psychology graduates has been widely discussed".

Readers of an academic article would probably find no problems with this sentence. The implications are clear: in a paper by one academic addressed to other academics, it will be understood that the discussions have been among other interested academics; where discussions have been broader (e.g. among employers), this will emerge from the list of supporting references.

Readers of a feature article, on the other hand, would have no such assumptions to guide them. Turn the sentence into the active voice, and it will immediately become apparent that the writer needs to explain who has been discussing this issue – is it employers? teachers? graduate psychologists themselves?

And what about that term "employability"? What exactly does it mean? Again, while academics may have a shared background of research which defines the term for them, readers outside academia might interpret it variously as "do psychology graduates make good employees?" or "does psychology give graduates something special that helps them get jobs?" or "do psychology graduates tend to be unemployed?"

Feature writing requires clarity. Ambiguities in meaning leap off the page: the more simply you write, the greater the clarity you need in your thinking.

One approach which may help if you wish to write features is to eschew standard academic headings (Introduction, Method, Discussion), even if you are reporting original research. Instead, think of a subheading which describes what the subsequent paragraphs are about. You will see that this is what I have done in this article.

Use of References

Some readers used to think that references are banned from feature articles, and then felt aggrieved when they found certain articles were followed by fairly lengthy lists! Let me explain.

In standard academic writing, references are used in two ways: (a) to establish the bonafides of the author (s/he has done the essential research, is familiar with the field); (b) to refer to published work which is central to the argument being presented. In feature writing, (a) is not required: our elaborate review process will establish the author's requisite knowledge of the field, and publication by **The Psychologist** is taken to establish the writer's expertise; (b) however may well be needed.

Reference to published work is more difficult and complex in feature writing. Whereas in an academic paper, it is often sufficient simply to indicate sources by listing authors and dates inside brackets, in a feature you need to explain exactly what it is that the authors said that is relevant to your argument. When you have done this, it may not be necessary to give a formal reference at all.

Let us take as an example some classic work on the psychological assessment of deaf people. A paper on intelligence in deaf children might refer to Vernon's meta-analyses which show that the evidence does not support the widespread assumption that deafness goes with low intelligence. An academic paper, by its very nature, would require the author to include somewhere the reference Vernon (1974). A feature article, on the other hand, would probably require some elaboration of his findings that deaf people suffer from the same kind of destructive judgements as those who can hear but are unable to speak, and that researchers have no business equating "dumb" with "low IQ". Given this elaboration, a formal reference would not be necessary. The author and the editor would need to decide together whether readers would benefit if it were included in a reference list.

The aim of feature writing is communication. Writers are trying to convey information to as many potentially interested readers as possible. It is for this reason that references are kept to a minimum: they tend to break up sentences, and make it difficult for an unaccustomed reader to follow an argument. My preferred approach is to keep them out of the text – with readers being told what the authors originally said and why it is important – with "suggested reading" listed for those who would like to read further. There are no hard and fast rules, though.

Writing and Communication

I wrote the first draft of this paper at the request of many people who asked for a clear explanation of the differences between feature and academic articles. The question itself led to our querying the usefulness of the distinction and to the merging of the two concepts into a hybrid created for **The Psychologist** by psychologists: the academic feature. Articles now aim to combine the best of both approaches: all papers are reviewed by expert referees, as for all academic journals; in addition, papers are required to be accessible to readers outside the expert's field, so that rewriting may often be required.

Communication is not easy, and yet I have the clear impression that our contributors share our desire to improve communications among all who are interested in our subject. I think that standards of writing go up all the time. Furthermore, I think that many academics and professionals would like to communicate with others outside their fields, and that they welcome suggestions as to how to make their writing accessible.

Editors too need to learn new skills if they are to help authors develop ease in moving from academic or professional journal to a wider audience. Following a trial workshop last year, I now conduct, with a colleague, Writing Workshops designed to help people to write and edit. We hope that others interested in communicating to a wider audience will attend future workshops.

No one supposes that we succeed in achieving the aims set out above all the time. Writing is a craft, and like all crafts takes work, and work is no good unless you know what you want to achieve.

Remember: If you know why readers should stop and read your paper, and bear it in mind as you write, chances are they will.

Note: Dr Mapstone was the Founding Managing Editor of **The Psychologist,** the monthly Bulletin of the British Psychological Society. She is a Chartered Psychologist, and now a partner in The Mapstone Williams Partnership which advises on communications between people in all professions. She is also Editor of **The New Academic.**

Editing "Deafness"
by
Kenneth Jones

Sociology is the observation and description of social phenomena. Deafness is a social phenomenon, and it has been my experience whilst doing research that it is not well observed or described. That's the reason there should be a journal.

'Deafness' is jointly published by the British Deaf Association and the Alliance of Deaf Service Users and Providers (ADSUP), and was originally the Journal of the National Council of Social Workers with Deaf People. From being a 'members only' Journal 'Deafness' now has a circulation of about 700, and we estimate that at least three times that number read it.

Not everyone liked the title 'Deafness', but I wanted something that when it landed on people's desks said what it was immediately. Also, I didn't want to deny deafness, there's too much of that already, with phrases such as 'hearing impaired', and magazine titles which do little to prepare prospective readers for the contents.

There isn't much literature on the British deaf community, and 'Deafness' exists to fill this gap, to some extent at least. Whilst there are few people who can be expected to write books about deafness, there are many who could write articles, specially if they have the offer of 'editing' help. What we are trying to do is build up a body of knowledge. In particular it is important that this body of knowledge should describe the experience of deafness, either through research into the lives of Deaf people, or the first hand description of the experience of deafness by Deaf people themselves.

Harlan Lane says 'the forces of darkness are the paternalism of the hearing experts, the inertia of the universities and the apathy of the Deaf community'. There is a good reason for the apathy of the deaf community. Deaf people have been the 'cared for' and as Paddy Ladd has said, years of oralism have created many difficulties for them, particularly in the area of self advocacy.

The hearing 'experts' are beginning to show a modicum of humility, and some of the articles in 'Deafness' demonstrate this – though I must add that they have a long way to go. For example, we have a growing 'profession' of Interpreters, yet most of what is said about the provision of interpreting services is based upon anecdote, hear-say and supposition. The role of the Interpreter has been established, and Deaf peole are told how to use an Interpreter, yet there is no research which shows the need. Clearly, there is a need for interpreting hearing people to deaf people, and vice versa, but surely the need should have been established first, then the role made to fit the provision. As it is we are left with many unresolved issues.

The inertia of the universities is manifest in the lack of literature, though there are some honourable exceptions. We have to hope that the situation will improve as more Deaf people become professionals and academics; there is evidence in the pages of 'Deafness' that this is beginning to happen.

We have tried to address all the main issues in 'Deafness'; the plight of Deaf children and their parents, Black and Deaf, communication, personal social services, deaf culture and community; and the guest editorial is a sort of 'soap box' where writers can let off steam, and perhaps introduce a new idea.

Whilst I respect the English language, I have to say that as editor I am biased more to good ideas than literary skill. And I think it's necessary to do the minimum of 'tidying up', however crudely the ideas are expressed, in order to retain the original character. Though needless to say, it's a joy to receive copy from the Jim Kyles, Paddy Ladds and Susan Gregorys of this world.

Sadly, not many Deaf people read 'Deafness' because they don't have the English. In years to come things might be different if the education of Deaf children takes a proper hold of bi-ingualism, but in the meantime we should be looking at video as a means of enabling Deaf people to both contribute and 'read' the Journal. In Lincolnshire we've just started to video the Chaplain's newsletter, and it's not obvious that Deaf people can contribute their own ideas through this medium. If we can do it at this level, it should be possible to do it with 'Deafness', in part at least.

'Deafness' has snowballed; where once I was struggling for copy, and having to persuade people to contribute, I now find that people are, if not exactly eager, at least interested. It's been a great experience being editor and it becomes more interesting with each issue. We have to thank the British Deaf Association for 'Deafness'. It's a valuable possession, the only Journal of its kind in Great Britain, and Bernard Quinn and Sheila Gregory at the BDA have put a lot of enthusiasm into its continued existence.

Diversity and Solidarity in the Deaf Perspective
by
Mervin Garretson

As a long-time member of the American National Association of the Deaf, it has been my privilege to serve in a variety of capacities, as secretary-treasurer, vice president, president and as interim executive director. More recently, in taking over the editorship of the **Deaf American**, we have changed it from a monthly magazine to an annual monograph. The first three monographs were **Eyes, Hands, Voices: Communication Issues Among Deaf People**; **Perspectives on Deafness** and **Viewpoints on Deafness**.

Goals of this deaf consumer organization include enabling deaf people to "achieve their maximum potential through increased independence, productivity and integration into the community." The key role of language in reaching these aims is self-evident. The NAD has long accepted American Sign Language (ASL) as a language in its own right, fully deserving of respect because of its importance to deaf people.

However, NAD also publicly recognises that there are two languages in the American deaf community, ASL and English. They believe that individuals have the right to become fluent in both languages and to use whichever language or combination of languages best suits their personal requirements. The rich linguistic variety within the World deaf community justifies the liberal outlook of the NAD and by its vigorous existence belies the efforts of those who would prohibit, deny and censor deaf opinion and the means by which it is expressed.

This was brought home to us recently when asked to be editor of an international monograph on differing perspectives on deafness by the Deaf American journal of the NAD.

The monograph shared views, experiences and information which often appear to be conflicting, inconsistent and even downright contradictory. We wondered if readers would begin to ask "Just what does the NAD believe in, if anything?"

But an editor is not necessarily a censor and the monograph was not about what the NAD believes in but a compilation of the varied perspectives of over 30 writers who have had rather extensive involvement with deaf people. The issue is at the heart of the editorial process and inevitably gives rise to key questions about the nature of editorial policy and the responsibilities of an editor.

One obvious task of any editor is to determine what is acceptable for printing and what is not. Webster defines editing as:–

1)   preparing something for publication by selection, annotation and revision and
2)   governing the policy of a newspaper or periodical and deciding what to print.

Some publications have for their focus the promotion of their own private industry, product, bias or organization objectives.

Such publications rarely, if ever, publish an article or story that does not support their views or philosophy. The *Volta Review* may be one illustration. This publication of the Alexander Graham Bell Association for the Deaf almost never publishes anything on sign language or sign systems, presumably on the basis that it would not interest their readers and probably because they do not believe signs help to promote speech and speechreading. Another example would be *Modern Maturity*, a publication of the American Association of Retired Persons, which tends to focus on stories and articles appealing to people over 50, or so-called senior citizens. Certainly there is legitimacy in publications which advocate a single view or certain belief.

However, we recognize the deaf community as a highly heterogeneous group of people. Included in this group would be ASL users, capital-D Deaf community diehards, more moderate ASL/Sign English users and those preferring manually coded English signs.

Members of this international deaf community also include pure oralists who do not sign at all; a new breed of oralists who will sign upon occasion, normally hearing persons with valence into the deaf group – through marriage, family, friendships or profession – hard of hearing people who may or may not sign and other deaf people who have been completely swallowed by what they call "the great hearing world!"

It has been said that an editor is "personally and entirely responsible for the editorial contents of the paper, and he must not allow himself to be influenced to uphold opinions which are contrary to the conscience and conviction." We believe deaf people, their friends and colleagues, parents of deaf children and all others have the right to a free press which implies a right to know all aspects of a very complex population.

We are interested in offering through *The Deaf American* a broad spectrum of views, information and experiences of both deaf and hearing persons involved with deaf people. We do not wish our constituents to end up like the people of Iraq who thought they were winning The Persian Gulf War because they were exposed to only one kind of misinformation!

Face to Face with John Hay
by
Pauline Jordan

John Hay is the author of the Face to Face column of the British Deaf News, he has interviewed various people over the past five years. Now it is his turn to be in the hot seat.

P   Good Morning Mr Hay. It gives me great pleasure to turn the tables on such a well known interviewer.

J   Good Morning Pauline. I clearly remember your TV interview of Mr John Major when he visited Donaldson's and told reporters that you were "very tough" and that his ordinary press interviews were easier. He said he was very impressed by you and your new generation of well-educated deaf children. I hope you will be kinder when interviewing a fellow deaf victim.

P   Absolutely gentle. Let me soften you up with some cosy questions about your family.

J   Good. I have only one.

P   What are the ages of your sons, Gordon and David?

J   Gordon will be twelve this July and David will be nine this June. Gordon shares the same birthsign, Cancer, as me! Both boys were born profoundly Deaf. Gordon was one of the first babies to be assessed on the new computerised audiometric cot at Simpson's Memorial Maternity Pavilion in Edinburgh. David was assessed on the same machine for the TV Deaf programme "See Hear".

P   From your experiences of raising two Deaf boys, what do you consider to be the most important aspect in the development of a Deaf child?

J   Of course, the most important aspect is communication, to have eye to eye contact, and to be introduced to many people as possible so that the Deaf child sees different people and different communication methods, that is one aspect that I missed in my time.

P   Do your sons integrate much with other hearing children?

J   When the boys were very young, they went to the local mothers' and toddlers' group and played with other boys, but now the boys are conscious that they are Deaf. They do play with the other children in the neighbourhood. One girls in the neighbourhood can sign, so the children integrate through signing. David has two friends his age who parents are former houseparents at Donaldson's College. Gordon and David both go to the local Boy's Brigade at Murrayfield Parish Church. Gordon enjoys it because of the physical activity, he is often asked to play in a representative football match. The boys integrate well with their hearing cousins who again come from a Deaf family.

P   At present, your sons both attend my school, Donaldson's College, in Edinburgh. Are you considering sending them to your former school, Mary Hare Grammar School in Newbury?

J   At the moment, Gordon is at the age. He should start Secondary at the beginning of the next academic year. As my hero Winston Churchill once said that he disliked his time in public school, I can see some drawbacks. As a former pupil, I might imagine Mary Hare as a suitable school for Gordon. Recently, Donaldson's College has introduced school leaving examinations which were not available in my day and I know that you yourself Pauline have already got University entrance before leaving school and will begin to study Maths and Computer Science at Edinburgh University this year. My wife and I must look into this situation. We are evaluating whether Gordon can fit in at Mary Hare or stay at Donaldson's. Both schools present pupils for Certificate Examinations but with different methods, Oralism at Mary Hare compared with bilingual Signing at Donaldson's. Mary Hare has a wide range of subjects while Donaldson's is at the "Development Stage". It is a real dilemma for me and my wife. I must use my head not my heart.

P   I always thought your heart was against oral-only teaching. What are your hopes for Gordon and David's futures?

J   Like all parents, we hope both boys' futures will be happy careerwise and socially. It's not good to pressure them to do what we expect, if they want to go on to Higher Education. It is important that they do what they are happy in.

P   How did you meet your wife, Shirley?

J   The Deaf world is a very small one. It is possible to know everyone by meeting or hearing about them. I first saw Shirley at a Sports Day at Mary Hare. She came with her parents to see her sister, Rosemary, who was in my year group. I actually met her at the start of my first holiday with the British Deaf Tourist Movement, organised by Arthur Dimmock in 1970. We just had a platonic friendship. I met her again when she came to Edinburgh with her fiance. My brother and I acted as tour guides for Shirley and her fiance. I started to really get to know her when she moved to Glasgow. It was then I hooked her! I married her in October 1979 after a short engagement.

P   As one of the Governors of Donaldson's College, could you please tell me about the set up of the Donaldson's College Board of Governors?

J   I am a member of the Donaldson's Trust. I took over from my father in 1982. The Board of Governor's is established of fifteen members, half of these include representative Governors from other bodies eg, Church of Scotland, The University of Edinburgh, The Education Institute of Scotland, COSLA and so on. The rest are co-opted Governors which include individuals such as doctors, bankers, parents etc. It is a privilege to be a Deaf Governor but I don't think I am the first Deaf Governor in the UK. The full board meets at least three times a year, they have three committees, the first is the House and Property Council which I am sitting on, the second is the Finance Committee run by Business people and people with financial knowledge, the third is the Education Committee.

P   What kind of topics do you discuss with other Governors on the Board?

J   We discuss many different topics ranging from staffing to budgeting links with other bodies. We also discuss some specific issues ie, special needs which some of our pupils have – for example, how to overcome the problem of oral examination in some Standard Grade exams.

P   Recently, Donaldson's College has had it's name changed from Donaldson's School for the Deaf to Donaldson's College. Does this mean that Donaldson's College will also have a department of Further Education along with the Nursery, Primary and Secondary departments?

J   Yes, definitely a department of Further Education. The constitution of Donaldson's School for the Deaf has changed to enable anyone over eighteen to attend Donaldson's College.

P   What developments on the College side of Donaldson's College will occur and when?

J   That's a tricky question. Right now we are concentrating on the development of the residential facilities for the present residents to make it more homely. We see that as a good advancement to take in more residents from all over Scotland. About the development of Higher Education, we have done a feasibility study of the whole building which includes student accommodation. We are starting to sort out what types of courses would be provided on the college side. In my personal opinion, there are lots of good teachers who can act as support teachers or interpreters for students who might go to hearing colleges or universities around Edinburgh. I know the Principal, David Scott, has had experience of organising Further Education when he was just only a teacher. For example, he organised the teaching of Data Processing and is at liberty to prioritise development of individuals, whether young or old. As for when, the Governors are very keen to see that the dream of Donaldson's providing Higher Education, which started twenty years ago, become reality soon. Already there are adult sign classes and a printing training course for older students and it is now common for seniors to stay on for particular courses after the age of eighteen.

P   Did you attend Donaldson's as a child before attending Mary Hare Grammar School?

J   Yes. I started first at the Infant department in the Saxe–Coburg building in 1952. Firstly as a boarder, in those days all children boarded at school. Through strong protests from Edinburgh based parents in 1954, Donaldson's allowed Day Pupil admission in all three departments. When I became five, I was transferred to the Junior department at Henderson Row. With the new block being built at the back of the Donaldson's Playfair building. Half of the Junior department at Henderson Row was transferred to Donaldson's School. I spent two years in the Junior department at Donaldson's before moving to the Senior department for a year then I passed the eleven plus examination to enter Mary Hare Grammar School to join my brother. Of course, like most schools at that time, we had an oralist education.

P   Can you tell me about your responsibilities as the Chairperson of East of Scotland National Deaf Children Society?

J   To be the Chairperson of the East Scotland NDCS which is an association of the NDCS. The NDCS is a parent organisation group with special interests of Deaf children. Like many chairpersons of many organisations, we are responsible for the construction of the organisation to serve the needs of our members and families. Our region in East Scotland has an unique position of being able to employ paid workers at our offices. To do that, I am the keyholder. I have to attend the offices at least once a week to see to the two part time workers and also to deal with the correspondence and prepare the agendas for the monthly Committee meetings. Also, sometimes I have to discuss what our Society would do for families. From time to time, I represent East of Scotland in the Scottish Coalition Council which meets in Perth. We discuss issues that affect Deaf children all over Scotland.

P The NDCS has been known, in the past, to be strongly in favour of Oralism, what changes have occurred in the last twenty years?

J The NDCS was established in 1944, by parents who were concerned that there was only one option for the Education of Deaf children. That option was boarding schools. From that concern, parents saw the development of day school facilities. Parents thought that they would prevent children from signing which were traditionally acquired in boarding Deaf schools. So it can be true that in the past twenty years, more and more Deaf adults have spoken out about their experiences of being a NDCS child to new parents of Deaf children. In the past twenty years, I have seen more use of interpreters at local region meetings. When I started on the Committee, there was no official provision of interpreters. Thanks to vigorous campaigns from the National Union of the Deaf on Deaf rights, the NDCS became aware that Deaf people had the right of choice. The NDCS on the whole should be impartial on any communication methods available. We, in the NDCS, believe that one child is different from others. NDCS are slowly drawing in Deaf parents.

P As a Deaf Historian, from your research into the history of Deaf people, can you tell me your personal opinion on whether there are significant differences between the history of Deaf and hearing people?

J The biggest difference in the history of Deaf and hearing people is that the History of the Deaf is not appreciated by anyone, whether Deaf or hearing. The history of hearing people developed from that of Kings to the current Queen and the current trends of social history and local history. Deaf history is not published in textbooks. It is my onus to put this right for the benefit of all Deaf children and adults. Also, hearing history can be recorded through written papers plus word of speech and also the records are carefully preserved in archives and libraries where there is ease of access. Whereas in Deaf history it is not easily accessible, for example schools, Deaf clubs and perhaps in private houses. Also, Deafness is not wholly hereditary so the transmission of traditions and stories is broken.

P As the author of the British Deaf News's face to face column, you must have interviewed various Deaf people. Can you recall any memorable events?

J Gosh, it has already been five years since I started writing for that column. It must be nearly sixty people I have interviewed! You have just put me in an awkward position. I do find every event memorable, everyone I have interviewed is equally interesting, but if you insist that I find a memorable moment then it will have to be when I was at the House of the Legislative assembly in Toronto where I was privileged to be given a strangers' pass to witness two ASL interpreters in action for the benefit of one culturally Deaf member of provincial parliament, Gary Malbowski. He cancelled all of his appointments when he got the minicom call from me to his secretary. To my amazement, he knew it was me, thanks to his regular subscription to the BDN. His success of being elected to parliament in this century is really amazing. That thing would have been easily done in the 18th century when Lord Seaforth was elected to the House of Commons at the end of the 18th century and some others were elected to the French Assembly as Deputies.

P You seem to be a very busy man jetting all over the world! Do you have any time for your interests and hobbies?

J All the things I am involved in, are my hobbies. Those things result in a lot of papers all over my house! My desk is overflowing with lots of papers and books on Deaf things. I do manage to watch teletext television. Shirley is very able to keep me up to date with the coming and goings of soaps like Coronation Street and Brookside. I am keen to see Deaf characters in soaps. In my young days, I avidly followed Hearts. I travelled all over to see the away games. I did bravely raid the border to England for the Texaco cup match and friendlies. I did fly to Hamburg for the European Winners Cup. Being married and a responsible father, my football spectatoring is severely cut down!

P   That's very interesting. Oh! is that the time, I must fly! Thanks for being so patient while I asked you these questions!

J   Oh! it's nothing really, I have enjoyed myself very much. Bye for now!

P   Goodbye!

A Background to Production
by
Gordon Davidson

The Scottish Workshop with the Deaf

The SWD aims at bringing together deaf and hearing people under a predominantly deaf secretariat to work in cooperation on a number of projects aimed at the general welfare of the deaf community. Day and weekend workshops are held to discuss topics of mutual concern – employment, education, social services, communication, research, overseas & third world involvements, arts and crafts. Deaf people are given valuable experience of organisation at a manageable scale and SWD often acts as a springboard to permanent positions in larger deaf organisations. The workshop runs a small publications division which helps to spread information about deafness to counter the more usual misinformation in newspapers and to support BBC and Independent TV in their excellent sympathetic and realistic coverage of deafness.

Scottish Workshop Publications

Printing & Publishing is almost exclusively a visual and practical procedure and as such is a career area very well suited to deaf workers. When given the chance, deaf people often flourish and rise to high levels of achievement.

At the Edinburgh festival recently, a play "Children of the Silent Night" remembered the work of Helen Keller who despite being deaf and blind wrote scores of books and had films made of her life. But ordinary deaf people are not Helen Kellers and the reality is that unnecessary barriers often block the careers of deaf people who wish to work in the printing and publishing industry.

For example, because of their ability to communicate in a noisy letterpress machine room, printing used to be admirably suited to deaf machine operators. The government press in Washington DC was dominated by deaf stereotypers and letterpress operators. The American printers Union welcomed this and warmly accepted deaf members. It was much the same in Edinburgh until the end of World War Two. Up until then, the use of rapid fingerspelling in Donaldson's Hospital ensured employment in the huge 80-firm printing industry of Edinburgh. With the introduction of oralism, however, school leavers did not have the literacy and good spelling needed for the trades of compositor and stereotyper and with the introduction of written examinations for printing apprentices, the number of deaf printers accepted rapidly shrunk to zero. Both the Edinburgh Master Printers Association and the various printing Trade Unions maintained this system for decades, despite the fact that it is clear discrimination against able candidates as, since the introduction of teaching by the Total Communication method in 1980, deaf school leavers have good written work and keyboard skills.

It was as a result of this injustice that Scottish Workshop Publications ceased to use hearing printers and set up their own printing plant in Donaldson's College with the help of the government Training Agency and latterly of Lothian Edinburgh Enterprises Limited. Six deaf trainees have helped to run the printing "shop" and have learned the skills of typesetting, graphics, formatting and layout. Voluntary deaf workers have also engaged in the skills of publication and marketing. All this leads to qualifications and makes trainees widely known and employable. In this way history has turned a full circle as Donaldson's was founded by a wealthy Edinburgh printer and publisher, James Donaldson, who bequeathed his fortune to this end.

Some Publishers of Deaf Writing

The Scottish Workshop for the Deaf cannot be accused of an inward-looking parochialism as it draws information from a wide range of writers and publishers concerned with deafness-related subjects. Foremost among these have been the influential papers, books and journals of the British Deaf Association, the periodicals of the National Association of the Deaf in USA and the world opinion molding output of Gallaudet University Press. The following address list may be of use to readers wishing to establish links of their own:

American Society for Deaf Children
East 10th & Tahlequah
Sulphur
OK 73086
USA

Breakthrough Trust
Birmingham Centre
Selly Oak Cottages
Bristol Road
Birmingham B29 6LE
UK

British Deaf Association
38 Victoria Place
Carlisle
CA1 1HU
UK

Carcanet Press
208/12 Corn Exchange Building
Manchester
M4 3BQ
UK

Creation Books
83 Clerkenwell Road
London
EC1M 5RJ
UK

Gallaudet University Press
Gallaudet University
Kendall Green
800 Florida Avenue NE
Washington DC 20002-3695
USA

World Federation of the Deaf
Rue Franklin 110
1040 Brussels
Belgium

National Association of the Deaf
814 Thayer Avenue
Silver Spring
MD 20910
USA

NDCS
45 Hereford Road
London W2 5AH
UK

National Union of the Deaf
288 Bedfont Lane
Feltham
Middlesex
TW14 9NU
UK

RADD
27 Old Oak Road
London W3 7AN
UK

RNID
Royal National Institute for the Deaf
105 Gower Street
London WC1
UK

Scottish Workship Publications
Donaldson's College
West Coates
Edinburgh EH12 5JJ
Scotland

Sense
The National Assoc for Deaf-Blind & Rubella Handicapped
311 Gray's Inn Road
London WC1X 8Pl
UK

Jabberwocky and Jargonese
by
George Montgomery

Technical, Scientific and Administrative
Terms used to describe aspects of:

Printing & Publishing
Academic Life
Real Estate
Education
Education of Deaf People
Psychology & Mental Health
Deafness
Labels for the Deaf
Euphemisms for All

Printing and Publishing Terms

Advance	A guarantee. A fee advance to an author before publication.
Ampersand	The symbol "&" meaning "and".
Back-up	Printing on the reverse of a previously printed page.
Black letter	Trade term for Gothic styles of fount.
Blurb	A publicity notice on the cover of a book praising it.
Bold	Type made blacker for emphasis.
Camera-ready	Script which has been proof-read and laid out as it will be in print.
Caps	Capital or upper-case lettering.
Captions	Brief descriptive text accompanying graphics
Colophon address and logo.	Note of ISBN, copyright and production details with printers
Contents	Text and Graphics are described usually giving page numbers.
Cut	Graphical break in the printed text.
Double-spread	Printed content extending over two adjacent pages as in centre-fold photographs.
Dropped-heads	Chapter titles placed below the top of a page.
Edition	Reprinting with updates and changes in the original script.
End papers	Blank pages at the front and back of a text.
Fount/Font	A style of calligraphy standardised for printing eg uncial founts with separate letters such as Greek, Cyrillic, Gaelic & Saxon. Cursive founts such as italics, copperplate with letters which may be joined.
Imposition	The sequencing of pages for printing which ensures that they will be in order when folded.
Impression	A printing or re-printing without alteration.
Indent	A blank space on a line to indicate a new section, paragraph or alternate line of poetry.
Orphan	A bottom line on a page which clearly belongs to the next page. Eg a title of a new section or diagram or the first line of a paragraph.

International Standard Number (ISBN)	The "identity" number allotted to each book for rapid world Book recognition and retrieval.
Justification	The spacing of words, letters and punctuation marks to ensure lines are of equal length. Originally a tedious process sometimes missed out for convenience, it is now a routine feature of computer printing programs.
List, backlist	The names of books produced by a publisher.
Proofs	The first trial print-outs submitted for corrections either as galley proofs or arranged by pages.
Press proofs	Corrected proofs ready for printing.
Run	The printing of a given number of book copies.
Type area	The space on a page available for printing.
Typos	Keyboard errors made when typing a manuscript.
Desk Top Publishing (DTP)	A small size computerised publishing complex based on a computer, a monitor and a printer.
Scanner	A machine which transforms graphics into computer memory suitable for printing.
Text wrap	A facility which sets out text to "wrap" around graphics in a number of different ways.
Clip-art	A collection of "ready to use" drawings which may be "imported" or placed into a document as required.
Spell-checker	The program used to check the spelling of computer generated scripts in English (American or real English) and (International) in other languages.
Mail merge	A facility which merges different files together eg a list of names with an envelope document.
Wysiwyg	What You See Is What You Get. Shows the operator exactly what will be printed out as he works.
Table editor	Enables quick production and/or editing of tables. Eg, table of contents, index etc.
Font & style palettes	Quickly changes fonts and styles (ie bold, italic) of selected text at a touch of a button.

Academic Usage : a key to Administrative Language and Alphabet Soup in the UK

Degree	The central award given at graduation. There are grades of intellectual excellence in degrees in this order:

Bachelor's Ordinary degree   B.A., BSc etc
Bachelor's Honours degree   graded 1st Class
                                          upper 2nd Class
                                          lower 2nd class
                                          3rd Class
                                          B.A. (Hons) BSc (Hons)   etc
Master's Degree   M.A., MSc etc
Doctorate   Ph.D, D.Phil, D.Lit etc

Department	Staff and students located together in area devoted to one subject, eg., French, Sociology, Mathematics. A head of department is usually a Professor.
Diploma	A certificate in a special subject, usually taking up less time than a degree, less demanding and reinforcing the general education with specialist, often occupational, knowledge.
Faculty	A cluster of departments with similar subjects, eg., Science, Social Science, Arts. A head of faculty is usually a Dean.
Faculty/Staff	Sometimes university teachers, lecturer and tutors are collectively known as faculty. More formally, a faculty is the administration assembly of all teaching staff. Some universities only use the word "staff" to describe technical and maintenance workers employed by them and refer to academic staff as members of faculty.
Graduation	The conferring of a degree upon the successful completion of a course. The fact that this is a beginning and not an end to education is indicated by the use of the term "Commencements" as a name for the graduation ceremony.
Matriculation	The procedure of admission to the University Community.
Semester	A half of the academic year.
Seminar	A larger, more formal, type of tutorial often with a programme of invited speakers.
Term	One third of the academic year.
Tutorial	A relatively small class of students discussing topics with a single tutor.

Vacation	The gaps between time-tabled education and lectures used for personally directed reading, research, field trips and temporary employment. It is a bad mistake to regard vacations as equivalent to school holidays.
ABRC	Advisory Board for the Research Councils
AUT	Association of University Teachers
CNAA	Council for National Academic Awards. A body which supervises the examination and teaching of degrees taken in colleges of higher education outwith University.
CUA	Conference of University Administrators
CVCP	Committee of Vice-Chancellors and Principals
ERA	Education Reform Act 1988
FTE	Full-time Staffing Equivalents
GU	Gallaudet University, Washington DC, USA. The longest established and most prominent of the world's institutions of higher learning for Deaf students.
NAAS	New Academic Appointments Scheme
NATFHE	National Association of Teachers in Further & Higher Education
OU	Open University. This is a tutor-based, television-presented correspondence course leading to degrees.
PCFC	Polytechnics and Colleges Funding Council
SOED	Scottish Office Education Department
UCCA	Universities Central Council for Admissions
UFC	Universities Funding Council

Real Estate: a Student's Guide to Euphemism, Out of Focus

Sophisticated city living	Next to a rowdy bar
Country feel in the city	Previous owner kept a cow in the basement
Old World charm	Has some woodwork. Dirt floors
Contemporary feel	Has no woodwork. Needs clearing
Wide-open floor plan	Previous owner removed supporting walls
Eat-in kitchen	Previous owner sealed door from kitchen to dining room
Euro-kitchen	Smells of garlic
Move right in	Has been unoccupied for five years, except for vagrants, vandals, and a herd of goats
Motivated seller	Has been on market 14 years. Owner has died
Opportunity	Quick, before it falls down
Convenient	Located on freeway entrance ramp
Neutral decor	No murals of nudes or Elvis
Move in easy	Front door missing
Bachelor pad	Red velvet walls. Smells like stale beer
Lots of built-ins	Previous owner nailed furniture to the floor
Cozy	No room larger than 9 by 6
Starter home	Foundation has been dug
Outstanding	Sticks out like a sore thumb
Grandma's house	No electrical improvements since 1926. Two-seater outhouse
Close to shops	Next door to auto salvage business
Tudor	Has back door and front door
150-amp service	Owner kept an arc welder in the living room
Tenant wants to stay	Evicting tenant is your problem
Newer windows	Old windows were smashed in a police raid
Security system	Neighbour has a very loud dog

Educational Terms in UK decoded

Deliver	To express as in a sermon without feedback
Educational Centre	A school
Educational Manager	A head-teacher
Educational Situation	A classroom
Initiative	A project
Personnel	I.A. for human beings
Teach	Delivery of a lesson with interaction from children/students
AHT	Assistant Head Teacher
BATOD	British Association of Teachers for the Deaf
CV	Curriculum Vitae. A record of personal career details usually used when applying for admission to courses or for employment.
EIS	Educational Institute of Scotland
FLTG	First Level Guidance Teacher (replaces register teacher throughout Secondary School.)
HRU	Human Resource Units. Impersonal Administrativese for school teachers.
HT	Head Teacher
NAG	Natural Auralist Group
NUT	National Union of Teachers
PAT	Planned activity time
PAT	Professional Association of Teachers
PSD	Personal & Social Development
PTG	Principal Teacher of Guidance
Soc and Voc	Social and Vocational Studies
TVE	Technical and Vocational Education
TVEI	Technical and Vocational Education Initiative
WE	Work Experience
WOW	World of Work

Terms used in Education of Deaf People

Manualism — The doctrine that claims that the educational treatment of all deaf children must be solely via the manual skills of fingerspelling and signing and any oral communication prohibited.

Oralism — The doctrine that claims that the educational treatment of deafness must be via the oral skills of speech and lipreading and any manual communication prohibited.

The Combined Method — This is an educational approach which supplements speech and lipreading with manual signs and fingerspelling.

The Simultaneous Method — This is a development of the Combined Method which further coordinates speech and manual communication, to the point at which they are largely simultaneous. The word-order of ordinary spoken language is taken as the pattern to be followed manually.

LRS Method — The "Listening, Reading, Speaking" method of teaching deaf children is most effective with those who can hear with the aid of class auditory amplification devices. The emphasis on the establishment of associative links between different modes of communicating language could be profitably emulated by other methods.

The Verbotonal Method — This is an attempt to teach the reception and production of speech in deaf children by devices which direct vibrations to the whole body via points on the arms, skull and trunk.

The Concentric Method — This is a technique for teaching vocabulary by progressively adding to an essential small core. This Russian idea was adopted by the English Makaton vocabulary grades.

The Dactyl-Oral Approach — Russian schools teach a finger alphabet before speech and early coordinate the two. One letter stands for one sound and this does not clash with ordinary Russian spelling which is largely phonetic. Eventually fingerspelling is discarded and speech emphasised in training.

PGSS — Paget Gorman Signed Speech is a code which gives each word a hand sign. Signs follow the ordinary word-order of spoken language. It is taught in a few schools but is not accepted by any adult deaf community.

Cued Speech — This is a form of communication which supplements the lip-configurations of speech with additional cues by hand positions. Vowels and consonants are cued simultaneously thus preserving synchronisation with speech. Hand positions are not alone meaningful so that attention to the lips is essential.

The Rochester Method	This is an educational approach which supplements lipreading, speech and reading of language with finger-spelling in the one-hand alphabet. Manual signs are prohibited.
Pure Oral Method	This is an educational theory which attempts to simulate in deaf children the natural development of language in hearing children. Hence reading and writing are not taught until some proficiency in lip-reading and speech have developed.
Oral Method	This is an educational theory which emphasises the primacy of the oral skills of speech and lipreading but, unlike the pure oral method, admits the value of the written word as a auxiliary language channel. Manual signing or finger-spelling is prohibited.
Total Communication	The use of a combination of speech, lipreading, fingerspelling, sign and written communication in the education of Deaf children.
Compensation	The largely mythical, common-sense idea that loss of ability in one sensory or motor area is offset by increased ability and acuity in other areas.
Prohibitionism	An illogical derivative of compensationism. The doctrine that claims that a given educational treatment or attainment is made more effective by the banning or abolition of some other educational treatment or attainment. For example, in the ancient East, the locomotor attainment of girls was restricted by mutilation in order to make them more effective in the domestic sciences and in some old English grammar schools, the English language was banned in order to promote attainment in Latin. Educators of the deaf have often resorted to prohibitionist practices. The pure oral treatment demands the early banning of reading in order to foster speech and lipreading; the banning of lipreading by making pupils wear "surgical" masks in order to foster the use of residual hearing has been applied in France and USA. The banning of signs to promote fingerspelling is a feature of the Rochester Method and the banning of all manual communication to foster speech and lipreading is a main feature of the oral method widespread in Britain. Investigations have shown that none of these communication abilities is negatively related and the banning of one does not have any general improving effect on others. In the immediate teaching situation, however, pupils cannot often attend to two subjects at once, so that it is natural to ban manual signs in a speech or reading lesson, just as it is natural to prohibit German in a French lesson and to prohibit speech in the reading room of a library. But from this latter, it does not follow that speech and reading are negatively related or that the reading ability of the public would be improved in general if Librarians insisted on the abolition of speech on all occasions outside as well as inside the library. Similarly, the manual and oral skills of language acquisition are not incompatible in the sense that abolition of

one leads to improvement in the other. There is no incompatibility other than the differences natural to any bilingual situation.

Authoritarian Personality

A pathological irrational state in which perceptions are seen in clear-cut two way choices without compromise, graduations or any middle ground. Social perceptions are in terms of friend and foe without any neutrals, ideas in black and white without any grey (Gilmour 1970).

Autism

A communication disorder where realistic perception of the world is diminished. Developmental autism in children is characterised by an absence of ordinary relationships with other people Often such children are so uncommunicative that speech is not developed and little evident response to hearing tests may also be a feature of autistic children. Thus they may be initially misdiagnosed as deaf despite the face that their absence of eye-contact makes them very unlike most deaf children who eagerly look for eye-contact.

Auralism, Natural Auralism Or Acoupaedics

The doctrine which gives sole emphasis to auditory input in the education of def children. Advocates of this approach refuse to accept that some children cannot hear. By neglecting or prohibiting visual input such as lipreading, sign, fingerspelling and written language they claim to "normalise" deaf children into hearing via amplification devices. Thus language will be acquired through the aural channel in the "natural" way. This method works quite well with blind children but deaf and hearing children acquire language in a inextricable mix of aural (auditory) and visual language in which social communication based on eye-contact is important (see Autism). Most hearing children lip-read naturally without being aware of it. To attempt to reduce language acquisition to a single, aural, channel, attractive as it is to the hearing aid industry, has little appeal to deaf people and is about as "natural" as a plastic banana.

Ameslan

American Sign Language

Auslan

Australian Sign Language

Augmented Signs

These are a collection of manual signs especially developed for further education subject instruction at Gallaudet.

PVS

Phoneme Visual System. This is a visual representation of speech sounds by means of cathode ray or neon tubes.

PMS

Phoneme Manual System. This is a manual representation of speech sounds used in conjunction with lipreading to aid the teaching of speech.

Bilingualism

The parallel development of linguistic competence in two languages.

Multilingualism	The development of linguistic competence in 3 or more languages.
Phoneme Transmitting Systems	The generic name for PVS or PMS systems.
Esoteric Language	A language understood by a few. Often used to describe the private manual sign systems which arise among deaf children taught by oral-only methods.
Exoteric Language	A language understood by many, usually the ordinary spoken mother tongue of a given country.
Gestuno	The vocabulary of signs agreed by all deaf national authorities in the United Nations, see ISL.
ISL	International Sign Language. The language derived from Gestuno and used by interpreters and administrators of the World Federation of the Deaf.
Aphasia, Dysphasia	Non-function of part of the central nervous system (brain) due to lesion after injury or due to some developmental or functional anomaly. Auditory aphasia (see central deafness and auditory imperception).
Alexia, Dyslexia	Central (brain) anomaly or malfunction, resulting in the imperfect perception of the written word.
Agraphia, Dysgraphia	Central (brain) anomaly or malfunction, resulting in inability to write.
Dysarthria	Central (brain) anomaly or malfunction resulting in inability to speak not to be confused with the speech handicap of deafness. The speech organs of almost all deaf persons are in good working order and the neural links with central speech areas intact if undeveloped and not atrophied by disuse.
Agnosia	A central (brain) anomaly or malfunction resulting in the loss of recognition of previously known information eg places, colours, faces. (Specific inability to understand,lipreading may be associated with latter in very rare cases.)
Apraxia, Dyspraxia	A central (brain) anomaly or malfunction resulting in the inability to carry out specific voluntary actions (excluding speech: see dysarthria). For example, finger apraxia would make manual communication impossible.
Acalculia, Dyscalculia	Central (brain) anomaly or malfunction resulting in ability to count numbers.

Teacher of the Deaf	A school teacher who is qualified in the ordinary way but who goes on to obtain further qualification in the special problems of deaf pupils. Additional qualification is usually obtained by passing appropriate examinations after one year's full-time study. Many teachers of the deaf cannot/do not teach deaf children but restrict themselves to the partially hearing.
Visiting Peripatetic Teacher of the Deaf	A teacher of the deaf who specialises in teaching deaf children who are not in need of the special education of a school for the deaf and who generally fit in reasonably well to life in an ordinary school.
VTHI	Visiting Teacher of the Hearing Impaired.
Interpreters	The mediation between deaf persons using sign language and others is rarely a task of simple translation. Almost always a complex problem of interpretation exists. In order to fulfil the role properly, interpreters need to have some specialist experience in areas in which they operate eg, Psychiatry, Medicine , Social Work and Law.

Psychology & Mental Health : Some key concepts and key words for interpreters.

Psychologist	Psychologists have a minimum qualification of a university honours degree in Psychology. Most go on to take further post-graduate diplomas in particular areas such as industry, education or mental health. Apart from the latter (Clinical Psychologists) who work with Psychiatrists in hospitals, psychologists are usually concerned with all human behaviour rather than only with mentally disturbed behaviour.
Syndrome	A grouping of symptoms which form a relatively stable and recognisable cluster often useful in diagnosis.
Psychometrics	The use of standardised psychological tests of human abilities such as intelligence, personality, memory and communication skills.
Psychopathology	Mental Disease or malfunction
Organic Disorder	Mental illness with a bodily basis
Functional Disorder	Mental illness with no bodily basis
Psychosis	Serious mental illness
Schizophrenic Psychosis	Disturbed senses, feelings, thoughts and communication
Depressive Psychosis	Acute despair Psychosis
Paranoid Psychosis	Persecution delusions: untrusting
Affective Psychosis	Disturbed feelings uncontrolled
Delusions	Unrealistic thoughts
Hallucinations	Like dreams when awake
Neurosis	Lesser mental illness
Affect	Feelings
Euphoria	"High" effect
Anxiety	Nervous worry
Anorexia/Bulimia	Serious eating problems such as refusing food, then overeating and vomiting.
Insomnia	Sleeplessness
Alopecia	Hair falls out
Labile	Fluctuating instability

Hysteria	Intense thoughts affecting the body
Perseveration	Mindless repetition
Compulsive	Involuntary thought or habit
Obsession	Recurring (involuntary) thoughts
Phobia	Irrational fear
Personality Disorder	Lesser mental abnormality
Psychopathic Personality	No moral stability
Inadequate Personality	Cannot cope with life
Aphasia	Disorder in language area of brain
Echoing	A mindless copycat imitation which greatly inhibits real communication. For example, repeating questions instead of answering them
Echolalia	Mindless imitation of speech
Echopraxia	Mindless imitation of actions
(Cerebral) Lesions	(Brain) wounds
Chronic	Forever
Behaviours	Behaviour
Experiental	Learned from Experience
Occupational Guidance	The procedure whereby suitable areas of employment, within the capacity of the client, are established. This is usually a joint decision between client and adviser involving attainment and aptitude tests and interviews. Some school-leavers do not formulate their own ambitions clearly or realistically enough to contribute much to the process of finding suitable work and deafness makes such people more dependent upon the adviser and the results of objective tests.
Psychiatrist	Psychiatrists are properly qualified medical doctors who specialise in mental disorders and take further studies and qualification in that field. Most are employed in mental hospitals and some work is undertaken in out-patient clinics.
Therapy	Course of treatment

Psychotherapy	Treatment by communication leading to more realistic awareness
Group Therapy	Treatment by communication within a group. Sign language communication is the basis of group therapy with signing deaf patients
Therapist	One who applies therapy
Counsellor	One who works with a patient to develop understanding and improvement of life circumstances
Occupational Therapy	Treatment by which patients are exercised physically and mentally with tasks demanding activity, skill and concentration suited to their ability.
Physio-Therapy	Treatment of bodily actions by special physical exercises, massage and radiation
Art Therapy	Treatment using the expressive, creative and rehabilitative potential in painting, drawing, pottery, sculpture and kindred artistic work
Drama Therapy	Treatment using the expressive, creative and rehabilitative potential in mime and drama
Behaviour Therapy	Treatment by systematic relearning to replace unwanted habits
Rational/Cognitive Therapy	Treatment by directing the attention to ineffective thought processes and correcting these into realistic, effective patterns

The Language of Deafness Studies

Residual Hearing

Few people are wholly deaf and the utilisation of the remaining hearing acuity by auditory amplification devices usually helps the improvement of speech production in deaf children. Only about one third of profoundly deaf children can exploit residual hearing to any useful extent. Dr James Kerr-Love in Glasgow first discovered that useful residual hearing exists in many people assumed wholly deaf.

Adventitious Deafness

When loss of hearing occurs later in life. The later deafened may have substantial language developed before the loss of hearing. Children who are post-linguistically deafened often do not require the special methods used to promote speech in those born deaf. Oral methods are more effective with children who have later or lesser deafness.

Partially Hearing

Partially deaf.

Deaf & Dumb

Early profound deafness often results in an inability to hear one's own voice. Without this ability, speech does not develop naturally and without speech, language development is delayed unless a visual language is acquired. Such people, traditionally labelled "dumb", usually prefer to be called simply "deaf". In American usage dumb implies a retardation in general not simply an inability to speak.

Hyperacusis

A sensation of pain associated with high intensity sounds; see Recruitment.

Recruitment

Acute usually painful sensitivity to sounds over a particular intensity threshold in perceptive deafness.

Threshold

The point of measurement above which a person responds to a stimulus.

Presbyacusis

A decline in hearing acuity associated with old age; usually occurring at the higher frequencies.

Decibel (dB)

(.1 of a Bel named after the inventor Alexander Graham Bell, an Edinburgh Teacher of the Deaf.): a logarithmic measure of sound derived from a reference point of sound pressure conventionally set at .0002 dyne per square centimetre. The human ear hears this as loudness.

Hertz (Hz)	(After the German Physicist). A measure of the wavelength of sound expressed as a frequency in cycles per second. The human ear hears this as pitch.
Ascertainment	The diagnostic process whereby the type, degree and onset of deafness, usually in childhood, is established and allocation to suitable treatment groups undertaken. Most profound deafness is irreversible and hence the only effective treatment is educational.
Audiologist	This is the profession concerned with the measurement of (residual) hearing by pure-tone and other audiometric devices and the recommendation of suitable artificial hearing aids.
Experimental Deafness	Temporary hearing loss imposed upon hearing subjects in an experiment. Isolation in a sound-proof cabin, masking or exposure to long periods of literally "deafening" noise all with or without occlusion of the external meatus have been used. The aim often is to study particular effects on skills and abilities of suddenly imposed hearing loss or a more general sensory deprivation by adding the experimental loss of the senses of vision and touch.
Occupational Deafness	Hearing loss due to continual exposure to noise in industry. For example, "boilermaker's dip" occurs in this trade resulting in an irreversible deafness at the specific frequency of the noise of hammering on boilers. Pop musicians (and their audiences to a lesser extent) incur irreversible hearing loss due to over-exposure to self-inflicted amplified noise which may hover around the pain threshold.
Acoustics	The science of sound.
Hearing Impairment	A vague trash basket term used to describe any kind of hearing difficulty. Every human being has some kind of hearing impairment, at birth when the perception of sound is not developed beyond the reflex level and auditory imperception is general and in old age when the inroads of presbycuses occur. "Hearing Impaired" school children are usually those studied by those who are too idle to define deafness more precisely. But the term is a useful generic to collectively describe more meaningful sub-groups such as deaf, partially hearing and hard of hearing groups. By confounding the deaf and partially deaf under the cloak of "hearing impaired" then it is possible to claim general success for treatments which only work with the partially deaf.

Central Deafness	A perceptive deafness where the reception of nerve signals from the inner ear is faulty due to damage or malfunction in the hearing areas in the temporal lobe of the brain (central nervous system). The peripheral hearing organs may be intact but deafness complete.
Peripheral Deafness	This is a perceptive deafness where the transmission of sound is stopped at the inner ear stage due to malfunction of the hearing receptors and where the hearing areas of the brain are intact but disconnected.
Auditory Imperception	The behaviourial condition associated with central deafness. In practice, some partial peripheral deafness is often present, perhaps due to the "occupational" deafness arising from educational treatment via classroom devices with amplification at or beyond 135 Db. Again as sound is not perceived, accidental prolonged exposure to intense noise may occur abusing the peripheral organs as would happen with a hearing person subjected to similar noise conducive to experimental deafness.
Paracusis	When a person with conductive deafness can hear better in noisy conditions than in quiet.
Békésy Audiogram	A self administered audiogram which continuously registers just above and below the intensity threshold of hearing in response to pure tones of increasing frequency presented in small increments from low to high frequencies.
Free Field Audiometer	An electrical audiometer which emits pure tones directly instead of through headphones as is more common. Free field audiometry obtains a generalised responses from both ears or either ear instead of the more usual controlled response from each ear measured separately.
TTS	Temporary Threshold Shift. The change in hearing acuity due to exposure to high intensity sound as in experimental and occupational deafness.
DAF	Delayed Auditory Feedback. The experimental intervention between a persons speech and his hearing of his own speech via headphones of an artificial delay. When the delay is between $\frac{1}{20}$ and $\frac{1}{40}$ of a second this induces stammering in the speech of a hearing person. This phenomenon may be used to diagnose malingering in hearing persons claiming to be deaf (perhaps after an accident in order to claim damages or financial compensation).

158

Warble Test	A fluctuating two–tone signal presented to a subject who has to discriminate between it and other single tones i.e. whether "flutter" or "fusion" of sound prevails. Flutter–fusion tests of hearing are equivalent to flicker–fusion tests of vision.
Audiometric Standard	The scale on which audiometers are calibrated. Former standards such as American Medical Association (AMA) and British Standard (BS) are now replaced by an International Standard (ISO).
Tensor Tympani	A muscle by which some people may guard against an anticipated loud noise by slackening the ear–drum.
Receptor	The bodily mechanism for receiving information from the senses and transforming it into a form suitable for transmission along nerves to the brain, eg eyes, ears, nose. More precisely the retina in the eye and the cochlea in the ear undertake much of the transformation function.
Cochlea	The receptor in the inner ear which transforms sound, via the vibrations of the middle ear, into neural impulses to the brain.
Cochlea Implant	An electronic tranducer placed inside or just outside the cochlea to stimulate hearing.
Cochlea Nucleus	A staging point where nerves from the cochlea are assembled before leading to the central hearing areas in the brain.
Rubella	German Measles, the effects of this virus infection are usually slight, except for unborn babies. Where an expectant mother has rubella in the first three months of pregnancy the developing retina and cochlea structures of her child may be damaged resulting in the birth of a deaf, blind or deaf–blind baby.
Oto–toxins	Poisons, due to viral infection, rhesus blood incompatibility, jaundice or drugs such as Thalidomide and abortion medicants. These may damage the developing cochlea before birth and result in congenital deafness. Thus, mothers to be are advised to avoid pep–pills digestion and cough medicines, quinine and even aspirin.
Congenital Deafness	Deafness at birth due to hereditary transmission or damage before or during birth.
Hereditary Deafness	(Familial) Deafness transmitted in a dominant or recessive form like any other characteristic from ancestral forebears through parents.

Aetiology	The conditions associated with the onset of illness. With deafness clear-cut, cause and effect is often difficult to establish with certainty.
Otologist	A medical practitioner who specialises in the surgery and pathology of the hearing mechanisms and allied structures of the ear. Otological examination is essential in any ascertainment of deafness as otologists alone of the ascertainment team can diagnose serious conditions needing surgery such as Ménières disease and acoustic tumours.
External Auditory Canal	(or meatus) in common language "the earhole". This is ended by the tympanic membrane forming a tube which resonates at about 500 Hz.
Mastoid Process	The bony lump behind the pinna, which is commonly only identified when infected.
Eustachian Tube	A canal leading from the middle ear down towards the nose and throat. Blockage of this tube by mucous during a cold or catarrh may depress normal hearing acuity.
Otitis Externa	An inflammation of the external meatus.} much reduced in
Otitis Media	Middle ear inflammation. } incidence since the } discovery of antibiotics by Sir Alexander Fleming of Darvel, Ayrshire
Tympanic Membrane	(Tympanum) in ordinary language "the eardrum". A tough skin-like covering separating the external meatus from the middle ear. This membrane transmits sound as vibrations to the mechanisms of the middle and inner ear.
Pinna	(Auricle) in ordinary language "the ear" and, more descriptively, "lug" in the vernacular. The outer structure.
Inner Ear	The part of the ear beyond the middle ear cavity wall. The inner ear contains the hearing, balance and receptors.
Middle Ear	(Tympanic Cavity). The section of the ear containing the ossicles and access to the mastoid process and the eustachian tube.
Internal Auditory Canal	(Meatus). The continuation of the auditory canal beyond the tympanum.

Ossicles	The small bones which form links in the mechanism which transmits sound to the inner ear.
Malleus	A hammer shaped ossicle in the middle ear.
Incus	An anvil shaped ossicle in the middle ear.
Stapes	A stirrup shaped ossicle in the middle ear.
Mobilisation of the Stapes	A surgical operation to restore hearing where loss is due to the immobility of ossicles damaged by disease.
Otosclerosis	Degeneration of the bones of the ear, eventually resulting in a conductive hearing loss.
Conductive Deafness	When the receptors of the inner ear are intact but damage to the transmission mechanism along the auditory canal occurs. A "muffled" partial deafness may occur.
Perceptive Deafness	When the receptors in the inner ear are non-functional or when transmission to the brain via the 8th cranial nerve is defunct.
Sensori-Neural Deafness	Perceptive deafness. Nerve deafness.
Hysterical Deafness	The rare condition where hearing loss is caused by a hysterical mental condition. Some cases of "combat fatigue" in front line soldiers suggesting a mental origin of deafness are likely to contain an element of "occupational" deafness due to exposure to the blast and noise effects of explosive barrages and bombardment.
SISI	Short Increment Sensitivity Index Test. An audiometric test of sensitivity to small change of intensity. Above average sensitivity is thought to indicate cochlear involvement in any hearing loss.
Speech Audiometry	A test of speech reception via controlled auditory amplification. A subject is requested to repeat words transmitted by headphones from a tape recorded list of phonetically-balanced words. Thus it is usually a test of speech production and hence inappropriate for deaf people who cannot hear or who cannot speak. The discrepancy between pure-tone and speech audiometry is very useful in the ascertainment of site and type of hearing loss in partially hearing children.

Phoneme Count	A measure of speech production in deaf children by means of a literal count of speech-sounds correct in two samples of speech which includes all the sounds in English at least twice.
Np	The original measure of sound based on natural logarithms after its inventor Napier an Edinburgh mathematician. This was replaced by decibels.

70 Labels for the Deaf: a list of Pigeon-holes, Euphemisms and Categorisations for Deaf People.

"Deaf people, as we shall see, are subject to an onslaught of labels and negative stereotyping which, at times, are barely disguised attempts to place them into neatly defined 'hearing' categories which erode their sense of self and therefore make them more manageable." (Corker, 1990)

deaf
the deaf
Deaf
deif
deaf and dumb
deafie
dummy
DODA (Deaf of Deaf Adults)
DOHA (Deaf of Hearing Adults)
Culturally Deaf
prelingually Deaf
postlingually deafened
deafened in adulthood
congenitally deaf
genetically deaf
acquired deafness
hereditary deafness
adventitious deafness
recessive deafness
lesser deafness
later deafness
later and lesser deafness
sensori-neural deafness
perceptive deafness
conductive deafness
central deafness
peripheral deafness
audiological deafness
occupational deafness
prevocational deafness
postvocational deafness
family deafness
tone deafness
word deafness
social deafness

marginal }
mild }
moderate }
severe } deafness
partial }
profound }
pre-natal deafness
peri-natal deafness
post-natal deafness
old age deafness
presbycusis
presbyacusis
decreasing hearing
weak of hearing
weaker hearing
weakened hearing
hard of hearing
soft of hearing
partially hearing
marginal }
mild }
moderate } hearing loss
severe }
partial }
profound }
audist
audistic
audiocentric
aurally challenged
auditory impairment
auditory imperception
hearing impaired
hearing handicapped
hearing defective
hearing deficient

EUPHEMISM		DECODER	
MEDICAL	**CYNICAL**	**KINDISH**	**HARSH**
Cognitive deficit	Cerebrally challenged	Slow learner	Idiot, imbecile
Strabismus	Gaze anomaly	Crosseyed	Cockeyed
Vision impaired	Visually challenged	Visually impaired	Blind
Hearing impaired	Aurally challenged	Deaf	Deaf and Dumb
Hearing unimpaired	Manually challenged	Hearing	Hearie
Down's Syndrome	Genetic anomaly	Down's child	Mongol
Cerebral Palsied	Physically differenced	Brain damaged	Spastic
Psychotic	Psychiatrically ill	Mental	Mad
Dyspraxic etc	Physically involved	Disabled	Cripple
Dyslectic	Orthographically challenged	Can't spell	Illiterate
Dyscalculic	Mathematically challenged	Can't count	Innumerate
Dysphasic	Speech disordered	Tongue tied	Dumb
Alopecia	Follicularly challenged	Thin on top	Bald
Senescent	Chronologically challenged	Senior citizen	Old
Deceased	Metabolically challenged	Passed away	Dead
Alcoholic	Problem drinker	Drunkard	Lush
Chronic narcosis	Substance dependant	Drug addict	Junky
Obese	Circumferentially challenged	Rotund	Fat
Excess adipose tissue	Avoirdupoisically challenged	Skin far from bone	Slob
	Delinquent	Crook	Hood
	Altitude impaired	Tall	Lanky
	Vertically challenged	Short	Midget
	Maturity impaired	Kid	Brat
	Parentally challenged	Illegitimate	Bastard
	Culinary impaired	Cookingly differenced	Can't boil water
	Euphemistically challenged	Disabled	Handicapped

BIBLIOGRAPHY

Andersson Y (1988) Categorization of Deaf People and Culture as a Resource in Mental Health Services. Proc 1st European Congress on Mental Health and Deafness. Rotterdam, Netherlands

Batson T & Bergman E (Eds) (1972) The Deaf in Literature. Merrill Centre Library

Braddock GC (1975) Notable Deaf Persons. Gallaudet University Press. Washington DC

Bragg BN (1989) Lessons in Laughter. Gallaudet University Press. Washington DC

Corker M (1990) Deaf Perspectives on Psychology, Language & Communication. Skill Publication

Dimmock AFD (1993) Cruel Legacy: an Introduction to the Deaf in History. SWP, Edinburgh

Dimmock AFD (1959) "Deaf Great". British Deaf News

Dimmock AFD (1989) "Sporting Heritage". SWP, Edinburgh

Dimmock AFD (1991) "Tommy". a Biography of the Distinguished Royal Deaf Artist A.R. Thomson RA, RP, RBA. SWP, Edinburgh

Erting C J, Johnson R C et al (1994) The Deaf Way. Gallaudet U.P. Washington DC

Gannon J R (1989) The Week The World Heard Gallaudet. Gallaudet University Press. Washington DC

Garretson M (1984) Flight 137. Fragonard Press MD. USA

Garretson M (1984) Words from a Deaf Child. Fragonard Press MD. USA

Garretson M (1984) for Bill Stokoe. Fragonard Press MD. USA

Gilmour R (1970) Shades of Gray. Hearing. RNID

Hay J (1991) Face to Face with Willard Madsen. British Deaf News

Hay J (1978) Courtesy, Humour and Adjustment to a Mad World. SWP, Edinburgh

Jepson J (Ed) (1992) No Walls of Stone. Gallaudet University Press. Washington DC

Kelsall J et al (1992) Maternity Care for the Deaf. SWP, Edinburgh

Lee R (Ed) (1992) Deaf Liberation. NUD, London

Legat M (1982) An Author's Guide to Publishing. Hale, London

Loman R P (1964) Bitterweed. Bella Vista Press. Arkansas. USA

Löwe A (1990) Errare Humanum Est. J Brit.Ass.Teachers of the Deaf. Vol 14 No 5

Madsen W (1973) Conversational Sign Language. Gallaudet University Press. Washington DC

McLeish A (1926) Ars Poetica. Boston. Mass

Miles D (1974) Gestures. Northridge. USA

Montgomery G & Laidlaw K (1993) Occupational Dissonance and Discrimination in the Employment of Deaf People. SWP, Edinburgh

Panara RF; Denis TB and McFarlane JB (Eds) (1960) The Silent Muse: Anthology of Poetry by the Deaf. Gallaudet University Press. USA

Stelle TW (1982) A Primer for Parents with Deaf Children. SWP, Edinburgh

Tiegel-Hanson A (1895) Overflow Verses. Merril Centre.Library. Gallaudet University. Washington DC

Van Cleve JV (1987) Gallaudet Encyclopeadia of Deaf People & Deafness. Gall.UP. USA
    "Periodicals" by Jack R Gannon
    "Specialised Print Media" by Jerome D Schein

White A et al (1993) Hitting the Headlines: a Practical Guide to the Media. BPS Books, London

Williamson A (1993) A Holythroat Symposium. Creation Books. London

Wright D (1969) Deafness: a Personal Account. Carcanet Press

EPILOGUE

Hail and Farewell

On the meeting of Murray Holmes and George Montgomery with David Edwards for the last time and Paddy Ladd for the first time: Eastbourne, England, 1977.

We clattered round the raucous rat–race,
Shuttled in a screaming jet–plane,
Surfed on an angry sea of words
While deep within, the shattered core
Called out for calm, beneath the smiling shell.

At last we left the seething throng
Escaped the blinding noise of unkind light
And sat in sober peace behind a quiet pint.

Then it was we watched David for the last time
Write the wisdom of his sturdy soul in the air about him.
He told of well–loved friends, long gone
Who fought their own Goliaths for the truth;
Of little men too big to be half–hearted
Besting big men too small to be whole–hearted.

With quiet pride, his quick hands brought to life
The old school, the old team, the bright days departed.
His slow hands healed with tender skill
The torn mother who wept about her distant son.
And when his tear–filled fingers faltered
The young faces stilled, awaiting,
Hanging on to his hands until the theme continued.

.... But now those world–worn hands have paused again
And we must wait forever for the Sign.

Time
by
Bilbo Monaghan
1911–1994

So the laurel fades
in the snowswept glades
Of flying years,
As the dreams of youth find
bitter truth
Of pain and tears;

Through the cheering mass,
let the victor pass
To find fate's thrust;
As tomorrow's fame writes
another's name
On drifting dust.

SUBJECT INDEX

Academic Writing 83–97, 94–97. 126, 127
Acting See Theatre
African Signs 90, 91
Alliance of Deaf Service Users and Providers 130
Alliteration 25, 26
Americans with Disabilities Act 42, 89, 144–146
Anglo–Saxon 85, 89, 91
Art 1, 64–66
Auditory Training 79
Australian English 86

Banquets 120
Bede's Chronicles 76, 77
Berlin Institution for the Deaf 61
Bias 98–102
Bible 76
Black Deaf 89, 105, 130
Blindness 24, 104, 140
Bodhran 2
Bon Accord 1
Braidwood 57, 67, 78, 106
British Association of Teachers of the Deaf 82
British Broadcasting Corporation 91, 123, 126
British Deaf Association 115, 122, 130
British Library 116
British Psychological Society 125
Bulgaria 78

Central Institute for the Deaf 58
Charter of Rights, see Rights
Cochlear Implants 105
Code Napoléon 120
Communciation 9–10, 32, 76, 105, 125, 126, 129
Culture (Deaf) 1, 40
Cyrillic Alphabet 78

Daleks 116
Deaf/Blind 103, 140
Deaf Children 30–36, 39
Deaf Liberation 1, 115

Deaf Mosaic 42
Deaf Museum 42
Deafness Jargon 148–152, 163
Deaf Politicians 137
Deaf President Now 42, 123
Deaf Professionals 81, 137
Deaf Studies 83, 103
Deaf Utopia 79
Donaldson's College 1, 134–136
Duncannon Murals 65–66
Dunkirk 76, 82

Editing 125, 130, 132
Education 31, 53, 82, 147
Egyptian Study 46
Elaborated Language 85
Encyclopaedia of Deafness 41
Essay Writing 92, 95
Eugenics 88, 106
Euphemism 86–88, 164

Fame 170
Fate 170
Feature Writing 128
Fingerspelling 121, 149
Football 138, 169

Gallaudet University 4, 42, 74, 83, 140
General Teaching Council 82
Goliath 168

Haikus 26–28
Hearing Research Trust 34
Heritage 41
History 2, 40–63, 61, 137

Inclusion   SEE Mainstreaming
Indian Study 49
Integration SEE Mainstreaming
International Congress on Education of the Deaf 58, 116
Isolation Experiments 46–52 see also Mainstreaming

Japanese Signs 85
Jargons 141–164

Kendall Demonstration Elementary School 41
King of France 119

Lexical Imports 85, 119
Liberation 115–118
Linguistics 107, 122
Lipreading 57, 58

Mainstreaming 11, 43–44, 56, 58, 81
Manchester 83, 87, 116
Maternity Care 1, 34–35
Mental Health 153
Metaphor 25
Midwives for the Deaf 1, 35
Milan 57, 74, 76, 79, 103, 106, 116, 120
Moray House College 37
Music 2, 23, 69–72

National Association of the Deaf 41, 132
National Captioning Institute 42
National Deaf Children's Society 136–137
National Information Center on Deafness 44
National Theatre of the Deaf 4
National Union of the Deaf 115–118

Odes 29
Oralism 61, 64, 78, 107, 121, 149
Oscar 41
Oz 86

Paternalism 119
Pilgrim Fathers 65
Plosives 26, 27
Poetry 6–22
Political Correctness 87–91, 112–114, 164
Printing 139, 142, 143

Queen Elizabeth 64, 65
Queen of Scots 16

Real Estate 146
References 128
Restricted Language 85
Rhapsodies 28
Rhyme 24, 29
Rhythm 23, 29
Rights 118, 120
Royal Academy 64, 65
Royal Air Forc 64, 65c
Royal National Institute for the Deaf 83, 118, 123, 124

Samizdat 119–124
Scottish Study 48
Scottish Workshop with the Deaf 117, 122, 139
Sculpture 41
See Hear 134
Sicilian Study 47
Signes Naturelle 120
Sign Language 44–45, 74, 76, 80, 103
Sign Workshops 5
Sociology 130
Speechreading, see Lipreading
Speech Teaching 80, 116
Strathclyde 1

Talmud 77
Television Writing 4, 98, 103, 29, 42
Theatre 4, 5, 67, 68
Therapy 155
Total Communication 1, 107

University 81, 85, 94
Usher's Syndrome 103, 104

Victorian School for the Deaf 55, 86
Volta Review 57, 58, 132

Warnock Report 107
Women 110, 112–114
World Federation of the Deaf 37, 44, 91, 123